THE ESSENTIAL POEMS

ROBERT HENRYSON

Copyright © this edition Will Jonson

First Edition, 2013

ISBN: 978-1492739821

The author has asserted their moral right under the Copyright, Designs and Patents Act, 1988, to be identified as the author of this work. All rights reserved.

CONTENTS

The Prologue to the Moral Fables	5
The Cock and the Jasp	8
The Two Mice	13
The Cock and the Fox	25
The Fox and the Wolf	35
The Trial of the Fox	44
The Sheep and the Dog	62
The Lion and the Mouse	71
The Preaching of the Swallow	86
The Fox, the Wolf, and the Cadger	102
The Fox, the Wolf, and the Husbandman	116
The Wolf and the Wether	127
The Wolf and the Lamb	135
The Paddock and the Mouse	144
The Testament of Cresseid	154
The Complaint of Cresseid	172
The Laste Epistle of Creseyd to Troyalus	181
Orpheus and Eurydice	193
The Annunciation	220
The Abbey Walk	223

The Bludy Serk	226
The Garmont of Gud Ladeis	231
Against Hasty Credence	233
The Praise of Age	236
Ane Prayer for the Pest	237
The Ressoning betuix Aige and Yowth	244
The Ressoning betuix Deth and Man	245
Robene and Makyne	248
Sum Practysis of Medecyne	253
The Thre Deid Pollis	258
The Want of Wyse Men	260

The Prologue to the Moral Fables

Thocht feinyeit fabils of ald poetré
Be not al grunded upon truth, yit than,
Thair polite termes of sweit rhetoré
Richt plesand ar unto the eir of man;
And als the caus quhy that thay first began
Wes to repreif the of thi misleving,
O man, be figure of ane uther thing.

In lyke maner as throw the bustious eird,
Swa it be laubourit with grit diligence,
Springis the flouris and the corne abreird,
Hailsum and gude to mannis sustenence,
Sa dois spring thair ane morall sweit sentence
Oute of the subtell dyte of poetry,
To gude purpois, quha culd it weill apply.

The nuttis schell, thocht it be hard and teuch,
Haldis the kirnell, sueit and delectabill;
Sa lyis thair ane doctrine wyse aneuch
And full of frute, under ane fenyeit fabill;
And clerkis sayis, it is richt profitabill

Amangis ernist to ming ane merie sport,

To light the spreit and gar the tyme be schort.

For as we se, ane bow that is ay bent

Worthis unsmart and dullis on the string;

Sa dois the mynd that is ay diligent

In ernistfull thochtis and in studying.

With sad materis sum merines to ming

Accordis weill; thus Esope said, I wis,

Dulcius arrident seria picta iocis. 1

Of this authour, my maisteris, with your leif,

Submitting me to your correctioun,

In mother toung, of Latyng, I wald preif

To mak ane maner of translatioun -

Nocht of my self, for vane presumptioun,

Bot be requeist and precept of ane lord,

Of quhome the name it neidis not record.

In hamelie language and in termes rude

Me neidis wryte, for quhy of eloquence

Nor rethorike, I never understude.

Thairfoir meiklie I pray your reverence,

Gif that ye find it throw my negligence

Be deminute, or yit superfluous,

Correct it at your willis gratious.

My author in his fabillis tellis how

That brutal beistis spak and understude,

And to gude purpois dispute and argow,

Ane sillogisme propone, and eik conclude;

Put in exempill and similitude

How mony men in operatioun

Ar like to beistis in conditioun.

Na mervell is, ane man be lyke ane beist,

Quhilk lufis ay carnall and foull delyte,

That schame can not him renye nor arreist,

Bot takis all the lust and appetyte,

Quhilk throw custum and the daylie ryte

Syne in the mynd sa fast is radicate

That he in brutal beist is transformate.

This nobill clerk, Esope, as I haif tauld,

In gay metir, facound and purpurat,

Be figure wrait his buke: for he nocht wald

Tak the disdane off hie nor low estate;

And to begin, first of ane cok he wrate,

Seikand his meit, quhilk fand ane jolie stone,

Of quhome the fabill ye sall heir anone.

The Cock and the Jasp

Ane cok sum tyme with feddram fresch and gay,

Richt cant and crous, albeit he was bot pure,

Fleu furth upon ane dunghill sone be day;

To get his dennar set was al his cure.

Scraipand amang the as be aventure

He fand ane jolie jasp, richt precious,

Wes castin furth in sweping of the hous.

As damisellis wantoun and insolent

That fane wald play and on the streit be sene,

To swoping of the hous thay tak na tent

Quhat be thairin, swa that the flure be clene;

Jowellis ar tint, as oftymis hes bene sene,

Upon the flure, and swopit furth anone.

Peradventure, sa wes the samin stone.

Sa mervelland upon the stane, quod he,

"O gentill Jasp, O riche and nobill thing,

Thocht I the find, thow ganis not for me;

Thow art ane jouell for ane lord or king.

Pietie it wer thow suld in this mydding

Be buryit thus amang this muke and mold,

And thow so fair and worth sa mekill gold.

"It is pietie I suld the find, for quhy

Thy grit vertew, nor yit thy cullour cleir,

It may me nouther extoll nor magnify,

And thow to me may mak bot lyttill cheir;

To grit lordis thocht thow be leif and deir,

I lufe fer better thing of les availl,

As draf or corne to fill my tume intraill.

"I had lever ga scrapit heir with my naillis

Amangis this mow, and luke my lifys fude,

As draf or corne, small wormis or snaillis,

Or ony meit wald do my stomok gude,

Than of jaspis ane mekill multitude;

And thow agane, upon the samin wyis,

May me as now for thyne availl dispyis.

"Thow hes na corne, and thairof I had neid;

Thy cullour dois bot confort to the sicht,

And that is not aneuch my wame to feid,

For wyfis sayis that lukand wark was licht.

I wald sum meit have, get it geve I micht,

For houngrie men may not weill leve on lukis:

Had I dry breid, I compt not for na cukis.

"Quhar suld thow mak thy habitatioun?

Quhar suld thow duell, bot in ane royall tour?

Quhar suld thow sit, bot on ane kingis croun

Exaltit in worschip and in grit honour?

Rise, gentill Jasp, of all stanis the flour,

Out of this midding, and pas quhar thow suld be;

Thow ganis not for me, nor I for the."

Levand this jewell law upon the ground,

To seik his meit this cok his wayis went.

Bot quhen or how or quhome be it wes found,

As now I set to hald na argument.

Bot of the inward sentence and intent

Of this fabill, as myne author dois write,

I sall reheirs in rude and hamelie dite.

Moralitas

This jolie jasp hes properteis sevin:

The first, of cullour it is mervelous,

Part lyke the fyre and part lyke to the hevin;

It makis ane man stark and victorious;

Preservis als fra cacis perrillous;

Quha hes this stane sall have gude hap to speid,

Of fyre nor fallis him neidis not to dreid.

This gentill jasp, richt different of hew,

Betakinnis perfite prudence and cunning,

Ornate with mony deidis of vertew,

Mair excellent than ony eirthly thing,

Quhilk makis men in honour for to ring,

Happie, and stark to wyn the victorie

Of all vicis and spirituall enemie.

Quha may be hardie, riche, and gratious?

Quha can eschew perrell and aventure?

Quha can governe ane realme, cietie, or hous

Without science? No man, I yow assure.

It is riches that ever sall indure,

Quhilk maith, nor moist, nor uther rust can freit:
To mannis saull it is eternall meit.

This cok, desyrand mair the sempill corne
Than ony jasp, may till ane fule be peir,
Quhilk at science makis bot ane moik and scorne,
And na gude can; als lytill will he leir -
His hart wammillis wyse argumentis to heir,
As dois ane sow to quhome men for the nanis
In hir draf troich wald saw the precious stanis.

Quha is enemie to science and cunning
Bot ignorants, that understandis nocht
Quhilk is sa nobill, sa precious, and sa ding,
That it may not with eirdlie thing be bocht?
Weill wer that man, over all uther, that mocht
All his lyfe dayis in perfite studie wair
To get science, for him neidis na mair.

Bot now, allace, this jasp is tynt and hid.
We seik it nocht, nor preis it for to find;
Haif we richis, na better lyfe we bid,
Of science thocht the saull be bair and blind.

Of this mater to speik, I wair bot wind,

Thairfore I ceis and will na forther say.

Ga seik the jasp, quha will, for thair it lay.

The Two Mice

Esope, myne authour, makis mentioun

Of twa myis, and thay wer sisteris deir,

Of quham the eldest duelt in ane borous toun;

The uther wynnit uponland weill neir,

Richt soliter, quhyle under busk and breir,

Quhilis in the corne, in uther mennis skaith,

As owtlawis dois and levis on thair waith.

This rurall mous in to the wynter tyde

Had hunger, cauld, and tholit grit distres;

The uther mous, that in the burgh can byde,

Was gild brother and made ane fre burges,

Toll-fre als, but custum mair or les,

And fredome had to ga quhair ever scho list

Amang the cheis and meill, in ark and kist.

Ane tyme quhein scho wes full and unfute-sair,

Scho tuke in mynd hir sister upon land,
And langit for to heir of hir weilfair,
To se quhat lyfe scho led under the wand.
Bairfute allone, with pykestaf in hir hand,
As pure pylgryme, scho passit owt off town
To seik hir sister, baith ovre daill and down.

Throw mony wilsum wayis can scho walk,
Throw mosse and mure, throw bankis, busk, and breir,
Fra fur to fur, cryand fra balk to balk,
"Cum furth to me, my awin sister deir!
Cry peip anis!" With that the mous culd heir
And knew hir voce, as kinnisman will do
Be verray kynd, and furth scho come hir to.

The hartlie cheir, Lord God! geve ye had sene
Beis kith quhen that thir sisteris met,
And grit kyndnes wes schawin thame betuene,
For quhylis thay leuch, and quhylis for joy thay gret,
Quhyle kissit sweit, quhylis in armis plet,
And thus thay fure quhill soberit wes their mude;
Syne fute for fute unto the chalmer yude.

As I hard say, it was ane semple wane,

Off fog and farne full misterlyk wes maid,

Ane sillie scheill under ane erdfast stane,

Off quhilk the entres wes not hie nor braid;

And in the samin thay went, but mair abaid,

Withoutin fyre or candill birnand bricht,

For comonly sic pykeris luffis not lycht.

Quhen thay wer lugit thus, thir sely myse,

The youngest sister into hir butterie hyid,

And brocht furth nuttis and peis, in steid off spyce;

Giff this wes gude fair, I do it on thame besyde.

This burges mous prunyit forth in pryde,

And said, "Sister, is this your dayly fude?"

"Quhy not," quod scho, "is not this meit rycht gude?"

"Na, be my saull, I think it bot ane scorne."

"Madame," quod scho, "ye be the mair to blame.

My mother sayd, efter that we wer borne,

That I and ye lay baith within ane wame;

I keip the ryte and custome off my dame,

And off my syre, levand in povertie,

For landis have we nane in propertie."

"My fair sister," quod scho, "have me excusit;

This rude dyat and I can not accord.

To tender meit my stomok is ay usit,

For quhy I fair als weill as ony lord.

Thir wydderit peis and nuttis, or thay be bord,

Wil brek my teith and mak my wame ful sklender,

Quhilk usit wes before to meitis tender."

"Weil, weil, sister," quod the rurall mous,

"Geve it yow pleis, sic thing as ye se heir,

Baith meit and dreink, harberie and hous,

Sal be your awin, will ye remane al yeir.

Ye sall it have wyth blyith and mery cheir,

And that suld mak the maissis that ar rude,

Amang freindis, richt tender, sueit, and gude.

"Quhat plesans is in feistis delicate,

The quhilkis ar gevin with ane glowmand brow?

Ane gentill hart is better recreate

With blyith visage, than seith to him ane kow.

Ane modicum is mair for till allow,

Swa that gude will be kerver at the dais,

Than thrawin vult and mony spycit mais."

For all hir mery exhortatioun

This burges mous had littill will to sing,

Bot hevilie scho kest hir browis doun,

For all the daynteis that scho culd hir bring;

Yit at the last scho said, halff in hething,

"Sister, this victuall and your royall feist

May weill suffice unto ane rurall beist.

"Lat be this hole and cum unto my place:

I sall to yow schaw, be experience,

My Gude Friday is better nor your Pace,

My dische likingis is worth your haill expence.

I have housis anew off grit defence;

Off cat, na fall, na trap, I have na dreid."

"I grant," quod scho, and on togidder thay yeid.

In stubble array, throw gers and corne,

Under cowert full prevelie couth thay creip;

The eldest wes the gyde and went beforne,

The younger to hir wayis tuke gude keip.

On nicht thay ran and on the day can sleip,

Quhill in the morning, or the laverok sang,

Thay fand the town, and in blythlie couth gang.

Not fer fra thyne, unto ane worthie vane,

This burges brocht thame sone quhare thay suld be.

Withowt God speid thair herberie wes tane

In to ane spence with vittell grit plentie:

Baith cheis and butter upon skelfis hie,

And flesche and fische aneuch, baith fresche and salt,

And sekkis full off grotis, meill, and malt.

Efter, quhen thay disposit wer to dyne,

Withowtin grace, thay wesche and went to meit,

With all coursis that cukis culd devyne,

Muttoun and beif, strikin in tailyeis greit.

Ane lordis fair thus couth thay counterfeit

Except ane thing: thay drank the watter cleir

In steid off wyne; bot yit thay maid gude cheir.

With blyith upcast, and merie countenance,

The eldest sister sperit at hir gest

Giff that scho be ressone fand difference

Betuix that chalmer and hir sarie nest.

"Ye, dame," quod scho, "bot how lang will this lest?"

"For evermair, I wait, and langer to."

"Giff it be swa, ye ar at eis," quod scho.

Till eik thair cheir ane subcharge furth scho brocht,

Ane plait off grottis and ane disch full off meill;

Thraf caikkis als I trow scho spairit nocht

Aboundantlie about hir for to deill,

And mane full fyne scho brocht in steid off geill,

And ane quhyte candill owt off ane coffer stall

In steid off spyce, to gust thair mouth withall.

This maid thay merie, quhill thay micht na mair,

And "Haill, Yule, haill!" cryit upon hie.

Yit efter joy oftymes cummis cair,

And troubill efter grit prosperitie.

Thus as thay sat in all thair jolitie,

The spenser come with keyis in his hand,

Oppinnit the dure, and thame at denner fand.

They taryit not to wesche, as I suppose,

Bot on to ga, that micht formest win.

The burges had ane hole, and in scho gois;

Hir sister had na hole to hyde hir in.

To se that selie mous, it wes grit sin;

So desolate and will off ane gude reid;

For verray dreid scho fell in swoun neir deid.

 Bot, as God wald, it fell ane happie cace:

The spenser had na laser for to byde,

Nowther to seik nor serche, to char nor chace,

Bot on he went, and left the dure up wyde.

The bald burges his passing weill hes spyde;

Out off hir hole scho come and cryit on hie,

"How fair ye, sister? Cry peip, quhair ever ye be!"

This rurall mous lay flatling on the ground,

And for the deith scho wes full sair dredand,

For till hir hart straik mony wofull stound;

As in ane fever trimbillit fute and hand;

And quhan hir sister in sic ply hir fand,

For verray pietie scho began to greit,

Syne confort hir with wordis hunny sweit.

"Quhy ly ye thus? Ryse up, my sister deir!

Cum to your meit; this perrell is overpast."

The uther answerit hir with hevie cheir,

"I may not eit, sa sair I am agast.

I had lever thir fourty dayis fast

With watter caill, and to gnaw benis or peis,

Than all your feist in this dreid and diseis."

With fair tretie yit scho gart hir upryse,

And to the burde thay went and togidder sat.

And scantlie had thay drunkin anis or twyse,

Quhen in come Gib Hunter, our jolie cat,

And bad God speid. The burges up with that,

And till hir hole scho fled as fyre of flint;

Bawdronis the uther be the bak hes hint.

Fra fute to fute he kest hir to and fra,

Quhylis up, quhylis doun, als tait as ony kid.

Quhylis wald he lat hir rin under the stra;

Quhylis wald he wink, and play with hir buk heid;

Thus to the selie mous grit pane he did;

Quhill at the last throw fortune and gude hap,

Betwix the dosor and the wall scho crap.

And up in haist behind the parraling

Scho clam so hie that Gilbert micht not get hir,

And be the clukis craftelie can hing

Till he wes gane; hir cheir wes all the better.

Syne doun scho lap quhen thair wes nane to let hir,

Apon the burges mous loud can scho cry,

"Fairweill, sister, thy feist heir I defy!

"Thy mangerie is mingit all with cair;

Thy guse is gude, thy gansell sour as gall;

The subcharge off thy service is bot sair;

Sa sall thow find heir-efterwart may fall.

I thank yone courtyne and yone perpall wall

Off my defence now fra yone crewell beist.

Almichtie God keip me fra sic ane feist.

"Wer I into the kith that I come fra,

For weill nor wo suld I never cum agane."

With that scho tuke hir leif and furth can ga,

Quhylis throw the corne and quhylis throw the plane.

Quhen scho wes furth and fre scho wes full fane,

And merilie markit unto the mure;

I can not tell how eftirwart scho fure,

Bot I hard say scho passit to hir den,

Als warme as woll, suppose it wes not greit,

Full beinly stuffit, baith but and ben,

Off beinis and nuttis, peis, ry, and quheit;

Quhen ever scho list scho had aneuch to eit,

In quyet and eis withoutin ony dreid,

Bot to hir sisteris feist na mair scho yeid.

Moralitas

Freindis, heir may ye find, will ye tak heid,

In this fabill ane gude moralitie:

As fitchis myngit ar with nobill seid,

Swa interminglit is adversitie

With eirdlie joy, swa that na state is frie

Without trubill and sum vexatioun,

And namelie thay quhilk clymmis up maist hie,

That ar not content with small possessioun.

Blissed be sempill lyfe withoutin dreid;

Blissed be sober feist in quietie.

Quha hes aneuch, of na mair hes he neid,

Thocht it be littill into quantatie.

Grit aboundance and blind prosperitie

Oftymes makis ane evill conclusioun.

The sweitest lyfe, thairfoir, in this cuntrie,

Is sickernes, with small possessioun.

O wantoun man, that usis for to feid
Thy wambe and makis it a god to be,
Luke to thy self, I warne the weill on deid.
The cat cummis and to the mous hes ee;
Quhat vaillis than thy feist and royaltie,
With dreidfull hart and tribulatioun?
Thairfoir, best thing in eird, I say for me,
Is merry hart with small possessioun.

Thy awin fyre, my freind, sa it be bot ane gleid,
It warmis weill, and is worth gold to the;
And Solomon sayis, gif that thow will reid,
"Under the hevin thair can not better be
Than ay be blyith and leif in honestie."
Quhairfoir I may conclude be this ressoun:
Of eirthly joy it beiris maist degré,
Blyithnes in hart, with small possessioun.

The Cock and the Fox

Thocht brutall beistis be irrationall,

That is to say, wantand discretioun,

Yyt ilk ane in thair kyndis naturall

Hes mony divers inclinatioun:

The bair busteous, the volff, the wylde lyoun,

The fox fenyeit, craftie and cawtelows,

The dog to bark on nicht and keip the hows.

Sa different thay ar in properteis

Unknawin unto man and sa infinite,

In kynd havand sa fell diversiteis,

My cunning it excedis for to dyte.

For thy as now, I purpose for to wryte

Ane cais I fand quhilk fell this ather yeir

Betwix ane foxe and gentill Chantecleir.

Ane wedow dwelt in till ane drop thay dayis

Quhilk wan hir fude of spinning on hir rok,

And na mair had, forsuth, as the fabill sayis,

Except off hennis scho had ane lyttill flok,

And thame to keip scho had ane jolie cok,

Richt curageous, that to this wedow ay

Devydit nicht and crew befoir the day.

Ane lyttill fra this foirsaid wedowis hows,

Ane thornie schaw thair wes off grit defence,

Quhairin ane foxe, craftie and cautelous,

Maid his repair and daylie residence,

Quhilk to this wedow did grit violence

In pyking off pultrie baith day and nicht,

And na way be revengit on him scho micht.

This wylie tod, quhen that the lark couth sing,

Full sair hungrie unto the toun him drest,

Quhair Chantecleir, in to the gray dawing,

Werie for nicht, wes flowen fra his nest.

Lowrence this saw and in his mynd he kest

The jeperdies, the wayis, and the wyle,

Be quhat menis he micht this cok begyle.

Dissimuland in to countenance and cheir,

On kneis fell and simuland thus he said,

"Gude morne, my maister, gentill Chantecleir!"

With that the cok start bakwart in ane braid.

"Schir, be my saull, ye neid not be effraid,

Nor yit for me to start nor fle abak;

I come bot heir service to yow to mak.

"Wald I not serve to yow, it wer bot blame,

As I have done to yowr progenitouris.

Your father oft fulfillit hes my wame,

And send me meit fra midding to the muris:

And at his end I did my besie curis

To hald his heid and gif him drinkis warme;

Syne at the last, the sweit swelt in my arme."

"Knew ye my father?" quod the cok, and leuch.

"Yea, my fair sone, I held his heid

Quhen that he deit under ane birkin beuch,

Syne said the Dirigie quhen that he wes deid.

Betuix us twa how suld thair be ane feid?

Quhame suld ye traist bot me, your servitour,

That to your father did sa grit honour?

"Quhen I behald your fedderis fair and gent,

Your beik, your breist, your hekill, and your kame -

Schir, be my saull, and the blissit sacrament,

My hart is warme, me think I am at hame.

Yow for to serve, I wald creip on my wame

In froist and snaw, in wedder wan and weit,

And lay my lyart loikkis under your feit."

This fenyeit foxe, fals and dissimulate,

Maid to this cok ane cavillatioun:

"Ye ar, me think, changit and degenerate

Fra your father and his conditioun.

Off craftie crawing he micht beir the croun,

For he wald on his tais stand and craw.

This wes na le; I stude beside and saw."

With that the cok, upon his tais hie,

Kest up his beik, and sang with all his micht.

Quod schir Lowrence, "Weill said, sa mot I the.

Ye ar your fatheris sone and air upricht,

Bot off his cunning yit ye want ane slicht."

"For," quod the tod, "he wald, and haif na dout,

Baith wink and craw, and turne him thryis about."

The cok, inflate with wind and fals vane gloir,

That mony puttis unto confusioun,

Traisting to win ane grit worschip thairfoir,
Unwarlie winkand walkit up and doun,
And syne to chant and craw he maid him boun -
And suddandlie, be he had crawin ane note,
The foxe wes war, and hint him be the throte.

Syne to the woid but tarie with him hyit,
Off countermaund haifand bot lytill dout.
With that Pertok, Sprutok, and Coppok cryit;
The wedow hard, and with ane cry come out.
Seand the cace scho sichit and gaif ane schout,
"How, murther, reylok!" with ane hiddeous beir,
"Allace, now lost is gentill Chantecleir!"

As scho wer woid, with mony yell and cry,
Ryvand hir hair, upon hir breist can beit;
Syne paill off hew, half in ane extasy,
Fell doun for cair in swoning and in sweit.
With that the selie hennis left thair meit,
And quhill this wyfe wes lyand thus in swoun,
Fell of that cace in disputatioun.

"Allace," quod Pertok, makand sair murning,

With teiris grit attour hir cheikis fell,

"Yone wes our drowrie and our dayis darling,

Our nichtingall, and als our orlege bell,

Our walkryfe watche, us for to warne and tell

Quhen that Aurora with hir curcheis gray

Put up hir heid betuix the nicht and day.

"Quha sall our lemman be? Quha sall us leid?

Quhen we ar sad quha sall unto us sing?

With his sweit bill he wald brek us the breid;

In all this warld wes thair ane kynder thing?

In paramouris he wald do us plesing,

At his power, as nature did him geif.

Now efter him, allace, how sall we leif?"

Quod Sprutok than, "Ceis, sister, off your sorrow.

Ye be to mad, for him sic murning mais.

We sall fair weill, I find Sanct Johne to borrow;

The proverb sayis, `Als gude lufe cummis as gais.'

I will put on my haly dais clais

And mak me fresch agane this jolie May,

Syne chant this sang, `Wes never wedow sa gay!'

"He wes angry and held us ay in aw,

And woundit with the speir off jelowsy.

Off chalmerglew, Pertok, full weill ye knaw

Waistit he wes, off nature cauld and dry.

Sen he is gone, thairfoir, sister, say I,

Be blyith in baill, for that is best remeid.

Let quik to quik, and deid ga to the deid."

Than Pertok spak, that feinyeit faith befoir,

In lust but lufe that set all hir delyte,

"Sister, ye wait off sic as him ane scoir

Wald not suffice to slaik our appetyte.

I hecht yow be my hand, sen ye ar quyte,

Within ane oulk, for schame and I durst speik,

To get ane berne suld better claw oure breik."

Than Coppok lyke ane curate spak full crous:

"Yone wes ane verray vengeance from the hevin.

He wes sa lous and sa lecherous,

He had," quod scho, "kittokis ma than sevin,

Bot rychteous God, haldand the balandis evin,

Smytis rycht sair, thocht he be patient,

Adulteraris that list thame not repent.

"Prydefull he wes, and joyit off his sin,

And comptit not for Goddis favour nor feid,

Bot traistit ay to rax and sa to rin,

Quhill at the last his sinnis can him leid

To schamefull end and to yone suddand deid.

Thairfoir it is the verray hand off God

That causit him be werryit with the tod.'

Quhen this wes said, this wedow fra hir swoun

Start up on fute, and on hir kennettis cryde,

"How Birkye, Berrie, Bell, Bawsie, Broun,

Rype Schaw, Rin Weil, Curtes, Nuttieclyde!

Togidder all but grunching furth ye glyde!

Reskew my nobill cok or he be slane,

Or ellis to me se ye cum never agane!"

With that, but baid, thay braidet over the bent;

As fyre off flint thay over the feildis flaw;

Full wichtlie thay throw wood and wateris went,

And ceissit not, schir Lourence quhill thay saw.

Bot quhen he saw the raches cum on raw,

Unto the cok in mynd he said, "God sen

That I and thow wer fairlie in my den."

Then spak the cok, with sum gude spirit inspyrit,
"Do my counsall and I sall warrand the.
Hungrie thow art, and for grit travell tyrit,
Richt faint off force and may not ferther fle:
Swyith turne agane and say that I and ye
Freindis ar maid and fellowis for ane yeir.
Than will thay stint, I stand for it, and not steir."

This tod, thocht he wes fals and frivolus,
And had frawdis, his querrell to defend,
Desavit wes be menis richt mervelous,
For falset failyeis ay at the latter end.
He start about, and cryit as he wes kend;
With that the cok he braid unto a bewch.
Now juge ye all quhairat schir Lowrence lewch.

Begylit thus, the tod under the tre
On kneis fell, and said, "Gude Chantecleir,
Cum doun agane, and I but meit or fe
Sal be your man and servand for ane yeir."
"Na, murther, theif, and revar, stand on reir.
My bludy hekill and my nek sa bla
Hes partit lowe for ever between us twa.

"I wes unwyse that winkit at thy will,

Quhairthrow almaist I loissit had my heid."

"I wes mair fule," quod he, "coud nocht be still,

Bot spake to put my pray in to pleid."

"Fair on, fals theif, God keip me fra thy feid."

With that the cok over the feildis tuke his flicht;

And in at the wedowis lewer couth he licht.

Moralitas

Now worthie folk, suppose this be ane fabill,

And overheillit wyth typis figurall,

Yit may ye find ane sentence richt agreabill

Under thir fenyeit termis textuall.

To our purpose this cok weill may we call

Nyse proud men, woid and vaneglorious

Of kin and blude, quhilk is presumpteous.

Fy, puft up pryde, thow is full poysonabill!

Quha favoris the, on force man haif ane fall;

Thy strenth is nocht, thy stule standis unstabill.

Tak witnes of the feyndis infernall,

Quhilk houndit doun wes fra that hevinlie hall

To hellis hole and to that hiddeous hous,
Because in pryde thay wer presumpteous.

This fenyeit foxe may weill be figurate
To flatteraris with plesand wordis quhyte,
With fals mening and mynd maist toxicate,
To loif and le that settis thair haill delyte.
All worthie folk at sic suld haif despyte,
For quhair is thair mair perrellous pestilence
Nor gif to learis haistelie credence?

The wickit mynd and adullatioun,
Of sucker sweit haifand the similitude,
Bitter as gall and full of fell poysoun
To taist it is, quha cleirlie understude.
For thy as now schortlie to conclude,
Thir twa sinnis, flatterie and vaneglore,
Ar vennomous: gude folk, fle thame thairfoir!

The Fox and the Wolf

Leif we this wedow glaid, I yow assure,

Off Chantecleir, mair blyith than I can tell,
And speik we off the fatal aventure
And destenie that to this foxe befell,
Quhilk durst na mair with miching intermell
Als lang as leme or licht wes off the day,
Bot bydand nicht full styll lurkand he lay,

Quhill that Thetes, the goddes off the flude,
Phebus had callit to the harbery,
And Hesperous put up his cluddie hude,
Schawand his lustie visage in the sky.
Than Lourence luikit up, quhair he couth ly,
And kest his hand upon his ee on hicht,
Merie and glade that cummit wes the nicht.

Out off the wod unto ane hill he went,
Quhair he micht se the tuinkling sternis cleir
And all the planetis off the firmament,
Thair cours and eik thair moving in thair spheir,
Sum retrograde and sum stationeir,
And off the zodiak in quhat degré
Thay wer ilk ane, as Lowrence leirnit me.

Than Saturne auld wes enterit in Capricorne,

And Juppiter movit in Sagittarie,

And Mars up in the Rammis heid wes borne,

And Phebus in the Lyoun furth can carie;

Venus the Crab, the Mone wes in Aquarie;

Mercurius, the god off eloquence,

Into the Virgyn maid his residence.

But astrolab, quadrant, or almanak,

Teichit off nature be instructioun,

The moving off the hevin this tod can tak,

Quhat influence and constellatioun

Wes lyke to fall upon the eirth adoun;

And to him self he said, withoutin mair,

"Weill worth my father, that send me to the lair.

"My destenie and eik my weird I watt,

My aventure is cleirlie to me kend,

With mischeif myngit is my mortall fait

My misleving the soner bot gif I mend;

Deid is reward off sin ane schamefull end.

Thairfoir I will ga seik sum confessour

And schryiff me clene off my sinnis to this hour."

"Allace," quod he, "richt waryit ar we thevis:
Our lyif is set ilk nicht in aventure,
Our cursit craft full mony man mischevis,
For ever we steill and ever alyk ar pure;
In dreid and schame our dayis we indure,
Syne `Widdinek' and `Crakraip' callit als,
And till our hyre ar hangit be the hals."

Accusand thus his cankerit conscience,
In to ane craig he kest about his ee,
So saw he cummand, ane lyttill than frome thence,
Ane worthie doctour in divinitie,
Freir Wolff Waitskaith, in science wonder sle,
To preiche and pray was new cum fra the closter,
With beidis in hand, sayand his Pater Noster.

Seand this wolff, this wylie tratour tod
On kneis fell, with hude in to his nek:
"Welcome, my gostlie father under God,"
Quod he, with mony binge and mony bek.
"Ha," quod the wolff, "schir Tod, for quhat effek
Mak ye sic feir? Ryse up, put on your hude!"
"Father," quod he, "I haif grit cause to dude:

"Ye ar the lanterne and the sicker way

Suld gyde sic sempill folk as me to grace;

Your bair feit and your russet coull off gray,

Your lene cheik, your paill and pietious face,

Schawis to me your perfite halines;

For weill wer him that anis in his lyve

Had hap to yow his sinnis for to schryve."

"A, selie Lowrence," quod the wolf, and leuch,

"It plesis me that ye ar penitent."

"Off reif and stouth, schir, I can tell aneuch,

That causis me full sair for to repent.

Bot father, byde still heir upon the bent,

I yow beseik, and heir me to declair

My conscience, that prikkis me sa sair."

"Weill," quod the wolff, "sit doun upon thy kne."

And he doun bairheid sat full humilly,

And syne began with "Benedicitie."

Quhen I this saw, I drew ane lytill by,

For it effeiris nouther to heir nor spy

Nor to reveill thing said under that seill.

Bot to the tod this gait the wolf couth mele:

"Art thow contrite and sorie in thy spreit
For thy trespas?" "Na, schir, I can not duid.
Me think that hennis ar sa honie sweit,
And lambes flesche that new ar lettin bluid,
For to repent my mynd can not concluid,
Bot off this thing, that I haif slane sa few."
"Weill," quod the wolf, "in faith thow art ane schrew.

"Sen thow can not forthink thy wickitnes,
Will thow forbeir in tyme to cum, and mend?"
"And I forbeir, how sall I leif, allace,
Haifand nane uther craft me to defend?
Neid causis me to steill quhair ever I wend:
I eschame to thig, I can not wirk, ye wait,
Yit wald I fane pretend to gentill stait."

"Weill," quod the wolf, "thow wantis pointis twa
Belangand to perfyte confessioun;
To the thrid part off pennance let us ga:
Uill thow tak pane for thy transgressioun?"
"Na, schir, considder my complexioun,
Seikly and waik, and off my nature tender;
Lo, will ye se, I am baith lene and sklender.

"Yit nevertheles I wald, swa it wer licht,

Schort, and not grevand to my tendernes,

Tak part off pane, fulfill it gif I micht,

To set my selie saull in way off grace."

"Thow sall," quod he, "forbeir flesch untill Pasche

To tame this corps, that cursit carioun,

And heir I reik the full remissioun.

"I grant thairto, swa ye will giff me leif

To eit puddingis, or laip ane lyttill blude,

Or heid, or feit, or paynches let me preif,

In cace I falt of flesch in to my fude."

"For grit mister I gif the leif to dude

Twyse in the oulk, for neid may haif na law."

"God yeild yow, schir, for that text weill I knaw."

Quhen this wes said, the wolf his wayis went;

The foxe on fute he fure unto the flude;

To fang him fisch haillelie wes his intent.

Bot quhen he saw the walterand wallis woude,

Astonist all still in to ane stair he stude,

And said, "Better that I had biddin at hame

Nor bene ane fischar, in the Devillis name.

"Now man I scraip my meit out off the sand,

For I haif nouther boittis, net, nor bait."

As he wes thus for falt off meit murnand,

Lukand about, his leving for to lait,

Under ane tre he saw ane trip off gait.

Than wes he blyith, and in ane heuch him hid,

And fra the gait he stall ane lytill kid.

Syne over the heuch unto the see he hyis,

And tuke the kid be the hornis twane,

And in the watter outher twyis or thryis

He dowkit him, till him can he sayne,

"Ga doun, schir Kid, cum up, schir Salmond, agane,"

Quhill he wes deid, syne to the land him drewch,

And off that new-maid salmond eit anewch.

Thus fynelie fillit with young tender meit,

Unto ane derne for dreid he him addrest,

Under ane busk, quhair that the sone can beit,

To beik his breist and bellie he thocht best;

And rekleslie he said, quhair he did rest,

Straikand his wame aganis the sonis heit,

"Upon this wame set wer ane bolt full meit."

Quhen this wes said, the keipar off the gait,

Cairfull in hart his kid wes stollen away,

On everilk syde full warlie couth he wait,

Quhill at the last he saw quhair Lowrence lay.

Ane bow he bent, ane flane with fedderis gray

He haillit to the heid, and or he steird

The foxe he prikkit fast unto the eird.

"Now," quod the foxe, "allace and wellaway!

Gorrit I am, and may na forther gang;

Me think na man may speik ane word in play,

Bot now on dayis in ernist it is tane."

The hird him hynt, and out he drew his flane,

And for his kid and uther violence,

He tuke his skyn and maid ane recompence.

Moralitas

This suddand deith and unpruvysit end

Of this fals tod, without contritioun,

Exempill is exhortand folk to mend,

For dreid of sic ane lyke conclusioun;

For mony gois now to confessioun

Can not repent, nor for thair sinnis greit,

Because thay think thair lustie lyfe sa sweit.

Sum bene also throw consuetude and ryte

Vincust with carnall sensualitie:

Suppose thay be as for the tym contryte,

Can not forbeir, nor fra thair sinnis fle.

Use drawis nature swa in propertie

Of beist and man that neidlingis thay man do

As thay of lang tyme hes bene hantit to.

Be war, gude folke, and feir this suddane schoit,

Quhilk smytis sair withoutin resistence.

Attend wyislie, and in your hartis noit,

Aganis deith may na man mak defence.

Ceis of your sin; remord your conscience;

Do wilfull pennance here; and ye sall wend,

Efter your deith, to blis withouttin end.

The Trial of the Fox

This foirsaid foxe that deit for his misdeid

Had not ane barne wes gottin richteouslie

That to his airschip micht of law succeid,

Except ane sone, the quhilk in adulterie

He gotten had in purches privelie,

And till his name wes callit "Father-war,"

That luifit weill with pultrie to tig and tar.

It followis weill be ressoun naturall,

And gre be gre off richt comparisoun,

Off evill cummis war, off war cummis werst of all;

Off wrangus get cummis wrang successioun.

This foxe, bastard of generatioun,

Off verray kynde behuifit to be fals;

Swa wes his father, and his grandschir als.

As nature will, seikand his meit be sent,

Off cace he fand his fatheris carioun,

Nakit, new slane, and till him hes he went,

Tuke up his heid, and on his kne fell doun,

Thankand grit God off that conclusioun,

And said,"Now sall I bruke, sen I am air,

The boundis quhair thow wes wont for to repair."

Fy, covetice, unkynd and venemous!

The sone wes fane he fand his father deid,
Be suddand schot for deidis odious,
That he micht ringe and raxe in till his steid,
Dreidand na thing the samin lyfe to leid
In thift and reif as did his father befoir,
Bot to the end, attent he tuke no moir.

Yit nevertheles, throw naturall pietie,
The carioun upon his bak he tais.
"Now find I weill this proverb trew," quod he,
"Ay rinnis the foxe, als lang as he fute hais."
Syne with the corps unto ane peitpoit gais
Off watter full, and kest him in the deip,
And to the Devill he gaif his banis to keip.

O fulische man! Plungit in wardlynes
To conqueis wrangwis guidis, gold, and rent,
To put thy saull in pane or hevines,
To riche thy air, quhilk efter thow art went,
Have he thy gude, he takis bot small tent
To sing or say for thy salvatioun.
Fra thow be dede, done is thy devotioun.

This tod to rest him he passit to ane craig,

And thair he hard ane buisteous bugill blaw

Quhilk, as him thocht, maid all the warld to waig.

Than start he up quhen he this hard and saw

Ane unicorne come lansand over ane law,

With horne in hand: ane buste in breist he bure;

Ane pursephant semelie, I yow assure.

Unto ane bank, quhair he micht se about

On everilk syde, in haist he culd him hy,

Schot out his voce full schyll, and gaif ane schout,

And "Oyas! Oyas!" twyse or thryse did cry.

With that the beistis in the feild thairby,

All mervelland quhat sic ane thing suld mene,

Gritlie agast, thay gaderit on ane grene.

Out off his buste ane bill sone can he braid

And red the text withoutin tarying.

Commandand silence, sadlie thus he said,

"We, nobill Lyoun, off all beistis the king,

Greting to God, ay lestand but ending,

To brutall beistis and irrationall

I send, as to my subjectis grit and small.

"My celsitude and hie magnificence
Lattis yow to wit, that evin incontinent,
Thinkis the morne with royall deligence
Upon this hill to hald ane parliament.
Straitlie thairfoir I gif commandement
For to compeir befoir my tribunall,
Under all pane and perrell that may fall."

The morrow come, and Phebus with his bemis
Consumit had the mistie cluddis gray;
The ground wes grene, and als as gold it glemis,
With gresis growand gudelie, grit, and gay,
The spyce thay spred to spring on everilk spray;
The lark, the maveis, and the merll full hie
Sweitlie can sing, trippand fra tre to tre.

Thre leopardis come, a croun off massie gold
Beirand thay brocht unto that hillis hicht,
With jaspis jonit, and royall rubeis rold,
And mony diveris dyamontis dicht.
With pollis proud ane palyeoun doun thay picht,
And in that throne thair sat ane wild lyoun,
In rob royall, with sceptour, swerd, and croun.

Efter the tennour off the cry befoir,
That gais on fut, all beistis in the eird,
As thay commandit wer withoutin moir,
Befoir thair lord the lyoun thay appeird:
And quhat thay wer, to me as Lowrence leird,
I sall reheirs ane part off everilk kynd,
Als fer as now occurris to my mynd.

The minotaur, ane monster mervelous,
Bellerophont, that beist of bastardrie,
The warwolff, and the Pegase perillous,
Transformit be assent of sorcerie,
The linx, the tiger full off tiranie,
The elephant, and eik the dromedarie,
The cameill with his cran-nek furth can carie.

The leopard, as I haif tauld beforne,
The anteloip, the sparth furth couth speid,
The peyntit pantheir, and the unicorne,
The rayndeir ran throw reveir, rone, and reid,
The jolie jonet, and the gentill steid,
The asse, the mule, the hors of everilk kynd
The da, the ra, the hornit hart, the hynd.

The bull, the beir, the bugill, and the bair,

The wodwys, wildcat, and the wild wolfyne,

The hardbakkit hurcheoun, and the hirpland hair;

Baith otter and aip, and pennit porcupyne;

The gukit gait, the selie scheip, the swyne,

The baver, bakon, and the balterand brok;

The fowmart with the fibert furth can flok.

The gay grewhound, with slewthound, furth can slyde,

With doggis all divers and different;

The rattoun ran, the glebard furth can glyde,

The quhrynand quhitret with the quhasill went;

The feitho that hes furrit mony fent,

The mertrik, with the cunning and the con,

The bowranbane, and eik the lerion.

The marmisset the mowdewart couth leid,

Because that nature denyit had hir sicht.

Thus dressit thay all furth for dreid off deid;

The musk, the lytill mous with all hir micht

In haist haikit unto that hill of hicht,

And mony kynd off beistis I couth not knaw,

Befoir thair lord the lyoun thay loutit law.

Seing thir beistis all at his bidding boun,
He gaif ane braid and blenkit him about,
Than flatlingis to his feit thay fell all doun;
For dreid off deith, thay droupit all in dout.
The lyoun lukit quhen he saw thame lout,
And bad thame, with ane countenance full sweit,
"Be not efferit, bot stand up on your feit.

"I lat yow wit, my micht is merciabill
And steiris nane that ar to me prostrait;
Angrie, austerne, and als unamyabill
To all that standfray ar to myne estait.
I rug, I reif all beistys that makis debait
Aganis the micht off my magnyficence:
Se nane pretend to pryde in my presence.

"My celsitude and my hie majestie
With micht and mercie myngit sall be ay.
The lawest heir I can full sone up hie,
And mak him maister over yow all I may:
The dromedarie, giff he will mak deray,
The grit camell, thocht he wer never sa crous,
I can him law als lytill as ane mous.

"Se neir be twentie mylis quhair I am
The kid ga saiflie be the gaittis syde,
The tod Lowrie luke not to the lam,
Na revand beistis nouther ryn nor ryde."
Thay couchit all efter that this wes cryde;
The justice bad the court for to gar fence,
The sutis call, and foirfalt all absence.

The panther, with his payntit coit-armour,
Fensit the court, as off the law effeird,
Than Tod Lowrie luikit quhair he couth lour,
And start on fute, all stonist and all steird,
Ryifand his hair, he cryit with ane reird,
Quaikand for dreid and sichand couth he say,
"Allace, this hour, allace, this dulefull day!

"I wait this suddand semblie that I se,
Haifand the pointis off ane parliament,
Is maid to mar sic misdoars as me.
Thairfoir geve I me schaw, I will be schent;
I will be socht and I be red absent;
To byde or fle, it makis no remeid;
All is alyke, thair followis not bot deid."

Perplexit thus in his hart can he mene

Throw falset how he micht him self defend.

His hude he drew far doun attoure his ene,

And winkand with the ane eye furth he wend.

Clinscheand he come, that he micht not be kend,

And for dreddour that he suld bene arreist,

He playit bukhude behind, fra beist to beist.

O fylit spreit, and cankerit conscience!

Befoir ane roy renyeit with richteousnes,

Blakinnit cheikis and schamefull countenance!

Fairweill thy fame; now gone is all thy grace!

The phisnomie, the favour off thy face,

For thy defence is foull and disfigurate,

Brocht to the licht basit, blunt, and blait.

Be thow atteichit with thift, or with tressoun,

For thy misdeid wrangous, and wickit fay,

Thy cheir changis, Lowrence, thow man luke doun;

Thy worschip of this warld is went away.

Luke to this tod, how he wes in effray,

And fle the filth of falset, I the reid,

Quhairthrow thair fallowis syn and schamefull deid.

Compeirand thus befoir thair lord and king,

In ordour set, as to thair stait effeird,

Of everilk kynd he gart ane part furth bring,

And awfullie he spak, and at thame speird

Geve there wes ony beist is in eird

Absent, and thairto gart thame deiplie sweir,

And thay said nane, except ane gray stude meir.

"Ga, make ane message sone unto that stude."

The court than cryit, "My lord, quha sall it be?"

"Cum furth, Lowrie, lurkand under thy hude."

"Na, schir, mercie! Lo, I have bot ane ee,

Hurt in the hoche, and cruikit as ye may se.

The wolff is better in ambassatry

And mair cunning in clergie fer than I."

Rampand he said, "Ga furth, ye brybouris baith!"

And thay to ga withowtin tarying;

Over ron and rute thay ran togidder raith,

And fand the meir at hir meit in the morning.

"Now," quod the tod, "madame, cum to the king;

The court is callit, and ye ar contumax."

"Let be, Lowrence," quod scho, "your cowrtlie knax."

"Maistres," quod he, "cum to the court ye mon;
The lyoun hes commandit so in deid."
"Schir Tod, tak ye the flyrdome and the fon;
I have respite ane yeir, and ye will reid."
"I can not spell," quod he, "sa God me speid.
Heir is the wolff, ane nobill clerk at all,
And of this message is maid principall.

"He is autentik, and ane man of age,
And hes grit practik of the chanceliary.
Let him ga luke, and reid your privilage,
And I sall stand and beir witnes yow by."
"Quhair is thy respite?" quod the wolff in hy.
"Schir, it is heir under my hufe, weill hid."
"Hald up thy heill," quod he, and so scho did.

Thocht he wes blindit with pryde, yit he presumis
To luke doun law, quhair that hir letter lay.
With that the meir gird him upon the gumis
And straik the hattrell off his heid away;
Halff out off lyif thair lenand doun he lay.
"Allace," quod Lowrence, "Lupus, thow art loist."
"His cunning," quod the meir, "wes worth sum coist.

"Lowrence," quod scho,"will thow luke on my letter,
Sen that the wolff na thing thairoff can wyn?"
"Na, be Sanct Bryde!" quod he. "Me think it better
To sleip in haill nor in ane hurt skyn.
Ane skrow I fand, and this wes writtin in -
For fyve schillingis I wald not anis forfaut him -
Felix quem faciunt aliena pericula cautum." 4

With brokin skap and bludie cheikis reid,
This wolff weipand on his wayis went,
Off his menye markand to get remeid;
To tell the king the cace wes his intent.
"Schir," quod the tod, "byde still upon this bent,
And fra your browis wesche away the blude,
And tak ane drink, for it will do yow gude."

To fetche watter this fraudfull foxe furth fure;
Sydelingis abak he socht unto ane syke.
On cace, he meittis, cummand fra the mure,
Ane trip off lambis dansand on ane dyke.
This tratour tod, this tirrant, and this tyke,
The fattest off this flock he fellit hais,
And eit his fill; syne to the wolff he gais.

Thay drank togidder, and syne thair journey takis
Befoir the king; syne kneillit on thair kne.
"Quhair is yone meir, schir Tod, wes contumax?"
Than Lowrence said, " My lord, speir not at me,
This new-maid doctour off divinitie,
With his reid cap can tell yow weill aneuch."
With that the lyoun and all the laif thay leuch.

"Tell on the cais, now Lowrence let us heir."
"This wittie wolff," quod he, "this clerk off age,
On your behalff he bad the meir compeir,
And scho allegit to ane privilage -
"Cum neir, and se, and ye sall haiff your wage."
Because he red hir rispite plane and weill,
Yone reid bonat scho raucht him with hir heill."

The lyoun said, "Be yone reid cap I ken
This taill is trew, quha tent unto it takis.
The greitest clerkis ar not the wysest men;
The hurt off ane happie the uther makis."
As thay wer carpand in this cais, with knakis,
And all the court in garray and in gam,
Swa come the yow, the mother off the lam.

Befoir the justice on hir kneis fell,
Put out hir playnt on this wyis wofully,
"This harlet huresone and this hound off hell,
He devorit hes my lamb full doggitly
Within ane myle, in contrair to your cry.
For Goddis lufe, my lord, gif me the law
Off this lurker!" With that Lowrence let draw.

"Byde!" quod the lyoun. "Lymmer, let us se
Giff it be suthe the selie yow hes said."
"Aa, soverane lord, saif your mercie!" quod he.
"My purpois wes with him for to haif plaid.
Causles he fled as he had bene effraid;
For dreid off deith, he duschit over ane dyke
And brak his nek." "Thow leis," quod scho, "fals tyke!"

"His deith be practik may be previt eith:
Thy gorrie gumis and thy bludie snout -
The woll, the flesche, yit stikkis on thy teith -
And that is evidence aneuch, but dout."
The justice bad ga cheis ane sis about,
And so thay did, and fand that he wes fals
Off murther, thift, and party tressoun als.

Thay band him fast; the justice bad belyif

To gif the dome, and tak off all his clais.

The wolff, that new-maid doctour, couth him schrif;

Syne furth him led and to the gallous gais,

And at the ledder fute his leif he tais.

The aip wes bowcher and bad him sone ascend,

And hangit him, and thus he maid his end.

Moralitas

Richt as the mynour in his minorall

Fair gold with fyre may fra the leid weill wyn,

Richt so under ane fabill figurall

Sad sentence men may seik, and efter fyne,

As daylie dois the doctouris of devyne,

That to our leving full weill can apply

And paynt thair mater furth be poetry.

The lyoun is the warld be liklynace,

To quhome loutis baith empriour and king,

And thinkis of this warld to get incres,

And gapis daylie to get mair leving;

Sum for to reull, and sum to raxe and ring,

Sum gadderis geir, sum gold, sum uther gude;
To wyn this warld, sum wirkis as thay wer wod.

The meir is men of contemplatioun,
Off pennance walkand in this wildernes,
As monkis and othir men of religioun
That presis God to pleis in everilk place,
Abstractit from this warldis wretchitnes,
In wilfull povertee, fra pomp and pryde,
And fra this warld in mynd ar mortyfyde.

This wolf I likkin to sensualitie,
As quhen lyke brutall beistis we accord
Our mynd all to this warldis vanitie,
Lyking to tak and loif him as our lord:
Fle fast thairfra, gif thow will richt remord.
Than sall ressoun ryse, rax, and ring,
And for thy saull thair is na better thing.

Hir hufe I likkin to the thocht of deid:
Will thow remember, man, that thow man de,
Thow may brek sensualiteis heid;
And fleschlie lust away fra the sall fle.

Fra thow begin thy mynd to mortifie,

Salomonis saying thow may persaif heirin,

"Think on thy end; thow sall not glaidlie sin."

This tod I likkin to temptationis,

Beirand to mynd mony thochtis vane,

That daylie sagis men of religiounis,

Cryand to thame, "Cum to the warld agane!"

Yit gif thay se sensualitie neir slane,

And suddand deith with ithand panis sore,

Thay go abak, and temptis thame no more.

O Mary myld, mediatour of mercy meik,

Sitt doun before thy sone celestiall,

For us synnaris his celsitude beseik

Us to defend fra pane and perrellis all,

And help us up unto thy hevinlie hall,

In gloir quhair we may se the face of God!

And thus endis the talking of the tod.

The Sheep and the Dog

Esope ane taill puttis in memorie

How that ane doig because that he wes pure,

Callit ane scheip unto the consistorie,

Ane certane breid fra him for to recure.

Ane fraudfull wolff wes juge that tyme and bure

Authoritie and jurisdictioun,

And on the scheip send furth ane strait summoun.

For by the use and cours and commoun style,

On this maner maid his citatioun:

"I, Maister Wolff, partles off fraud and gyle,

Under the panis off hie suspensioun,

Off grit cursing, and interdictioun,

Schir Scheip, I charge the straitly to compeir,

And answer to ane doig befoir me heir."

Schir Corbie Ravin wes maid apparitour,

Quha pykit had full mony scheipis ee;

The charge hes tane and on the letteris bure,

Summonit the scheip befoir the wolff, that he

Peremptourlie within twa dayis thre,

Compeir under the panis in this bill,

To heir quhat Perrie Doig will say the till."

This summondis maid befoir witnes anew,

The ravin, as to his office weill effeird,

Indorsat hes the write, and on he flew.

The selie scheip durst lay na mouth on eird

Till he befoir the awfull juge appeird.

The oure off cause quhilk that the juge usit than,

Quhen Hesperus to schaw his face began.

The foxe wes clerk and noter in the cause;

The gled, the graip at the bar couth stand,

As advocatis expert in to the lawis,

The doggis pley togidder tuke on hand,

Quhilk wer confidderit straitlie in ane band

Aganis the scheip to procure the sentence.

Thocht it wes fals, thay had na conscience.

The clerk callit the scheip, and he wes thair;

The advocatis on this wyse couth propone:

"Ane certane breid, worth fyve schilling or mair,

Thow aw the doig, off quhilk the terme is gone."

Off his awin heid, but advocate, allone,
The scheip avysitlie gaif answer in the cace:
"Heir I declyne the juge, the tyme, the place.

"This is my cause, in motive and effect:
The law sayis it is richt perrillous
Till enter in pley befoir ane juge suspect,
And ye, Schir Wolff, hes bene richt odious
To me, for with your tuskis ravenous
Hes slane full mony kinnismen off myne;
Thairfoir as juge suspect I yow declyne.

"And schortlie, of this court ye memberis all,
Baith assessouris, clerk, and advocate,
To me and myne ar ennemies mortall
And ay hes bene, as mony scheipheird wate.
The place is fer, the tyme is feriate,
Quhairfoir na juge suld sit in consistory
Sa lait at evin: I yow accuse for thy."

Quhen that the juge in this wyse wes accusit,
He bad the parteis cheis with ane assent
Twa arbeteris, as in the law is usit,

For to declair and gif arbitriment

Quhidder the scheip suld answer in jugement

Befoir the wolff; and so thay did, but weir,

Off quhome the namis efter ye sall heir.

The beir, the brok, the mater tuke on hand,

For to discyde gif this exceptioun

Wes off na strenth, or lauchfully mycht stand;

And thairupon as jugis thay sat doun

And held ane lang quhyle disputatioun,

Seikand full mony decretalis off the law,

And glosis als, the veritie to knaw.

Of civile law mony volum thay revolve,

The codies and digestis new and ald,

Contra et pro, strait argumentis thay resolve,

Sum a doctryne and sum a nothir hald;

For prayer or price, trow ye, thay wald fald,

Bot held the glose and text of the decreis

As trew jugis. I beschrew thame ay that leis.

Schortlie to mak ane end off this debait,

The arbiteris than summar and plane

The sentence gave, and proces fulminait:
The scheip suld pas befoir the wolff agane
And end his pley. "Than wes he nathing fane,
For fra thair sentence couth he not appeill.
On clerkis I do it, gif this sentence wes leill.

The scheip agane befoir the wolff derenyeit,
But advocate, abasitlie couth stand.
Up rais the doig, and on the scheip thus plenyeit:
"Ane soume I payit have befoir the hand
For certane breid." Thairto ane borrow he fand,
That wrangouslie the scheip did hald the breid,
Quhilk he denyit, and thair began the pleid.

And quhen the scheip this stryif had contestait,
The justice in the cause furth can proceid.
Lowrence the actis and the proces wrait,
And thus the pley unto the end thay speid.
This cursit court, corruptit all for meid,
Aganis gude faith, gude law, and eik conscience,
For this fals doig pronuncit the sentence.

And it till put to executioun,

The wolff chargit the scheip, without delay,

Under the panis off interdictioun,

The soume off silver or the breid to pay.

Off this sentence, allace, quhat sall I say,

Quhilk dampnit hes the selie innocent,

And justifyit the wrangous jugement?

The scheip, dreidand mair persecutioun,

Obeyit to the sentence, and couth tak

His way unto ane merchand off the toun,

And sauld the woll that he bure on his bak,

Syne bocht the breid, and to the doig couth mak

Reddie payment, as he commandit was;

Naikit and bair syne to the feild couth pas.

Moralitas

This selie scheip may present the figure

Of pure commounis, that daylie ar opprest

Be tirrane men, quhilkis settis all thair cure

Be fals meinis to mak ane wrang conquest,

In hope this present lyfe suld ever lest.

Bot all begylit, thay will in schort tyme end,

And efter deith to lestand panis wend.

This wolf I likkin to ane schiref stout
Quhilk byis ane forfalt at the kingis hand,
And hes with him ane cursit assyis about,
And dytis all the pure men up on land;
Fra the crownar haif laid on him his wand,
Thocht he wer als trew as ever wes Sanct Johne -
Slain sall he be, or with the juge compone.

This ravin I likkin to ane fals crownair,
Quhilk hes ane porteous of the inditement,
And passis furth befoir the justice air,
All misdoaris to bring to jugement;
Bot luke gif he wes of ane trew intent,
To scraip out Johne, and wryte in Will or Wat,
And swa ane bud at boith the parteis skat.

Of this fals tod, of quhilk I spak befoir,
And of this gled, quhat thay micht signify,
Of thair nature, as now I speik no moir.
Bot of this scheip and of his cairfull cry
I sall reheirs, for as I passit by

Quhair that he lay, on cais I lukit doun,

And hard him mak sair lamentatioun.

"Allace," quod he, "this cursit consistorie

In middis of the winter now is maid,

Quhen Boreas with blastis bitterlie

And frawart froistes thir flouris doun can faid;

On bankis bair now may I mak na baid."

And with that word in to ane coif he crap,

Fra sair wedder and froistis him to hap.

Quaikand for cauld, sair murnand ay amang,

Kest up his ee unto the hevinnis hicht,

And said, "O lord, quhy sleipis thow sa lang?

Walk, and discerne my cause groundit on richt;

Se how I am be fraud, maistrie, and slicht

Peillit full bair, and so is mony one

Now in this warld richt wonder wo begone.

"Se how this cursit syn of covetice

Exylit hes baith lufe, lawtie, and law.

Now few or nane will execute justice,

In falt of quhome, the pure man is overthraw.

The veritie, suppois the juge it knaw,

Thay ar so blindit with affectioun,

But dreid, for meid, thay thoill the richt go doun.

"Seis thow not, lord, this warld overturnit is,

As quha wald change gude gold in leid or tyn?

The pure is peillit, the lord may do na mis,

And simonie is haldin for na syn.

Now is he blyith with okker maist may wyn;

Gentrice is slane, and pietie is ago.

Allace, gude lord, quhy tholis thow it so?

"Thow tholis this evin for our grit offence;

Thow sendis us troubill and plaigis soir,

As hunger, derth, grit weir, or pestilence;

Bot few amendis now thair lyfe thairfoir.

We pure pepill as now may do no moir

Bot pray to the: sen that we ar opprest

In to this eirth, grant us in hevin gude rest."

The Lion and the Mouse

Prologue

In middis of June, that joly sweit seasoun,
Quhen that fair Phebus with his bemis bricht
Had dryit up the dew fra daill and doun,
And all the land maid with his bemis licht,
In ane mornyng betuix mid day and nicht
I rais and put all sleuth and sleip asyde,
And to ane wod I went allone but gyde.

Sweit wes the smell off flouris quhyte and reid,
The noyes off birdis richt delitious,
The bewis braid blomit abone my heid,
The ground growand with gers gratious;
Off all plesance that place wes plenteous,
With sweit odouris and birdis harmony;
The morning myld, my mirth wes mair for thy.

The rosis reid arrayit rone and ryce,
The prymeros and the purpour viola;
To heir it wes ane poynt off paradice,

Sic mirth the mavis and the merle couth ma;

The blossummis blythe brak up on bank and bra;

The smell off herbis and the fowlis cry,

Contending quha suld have the victory.

Me to conserve than fra the sonis heit,

Under the schaddow off ane hawthorne grene

I lenit doun amang the flouris sweit,

Syne maid a cors and closit baith my ene.

On sleip I fell amang thir bewis bene,

And in my dreme, me thocht come throw the schaw

The fairest man that ever befoir I saw.

His gowne wes off ane claith als quhyte as milk,

His chymmeris wes off chambelate purpour broun,

His hude off scarlet, bordowrit weill with silk

On hekillit wyis untill his girdill doun,

His bonat round, and off the auld fassoun,

His beird wes quhyte, his ene wes grit and gray,

With lokker hair quhilk over his schulderis lay.

Ane roll off paper in his hand he bair,

Ane swannis pen stikand under his eir,

Ane inkhorne, with ane prettie gilt pennair,

Ane bag off silk, all at his belt he weir.

Thus wes he gudelie grathit in his geir,

Off stature large, and with ane feirfull face.

Evin quhair I lay he come ane sturdie pace,

And said, "God speid, my sone," and I wes fane

Off that couth word, and off his cumpany.

With reverence I salusit him agane,

"Welcome, father," and he sat doun me by.

"Displeis yow not, my gude maister, thocht I

Demand your birth, your facultye, and name;

Quhy ye come heir, or quhair ye dwell at hame."

"My sone," said he, "I am off gentill blude;

My native land is Rome, withoutin nay,

And in that towne first to the sculis I yude,

In civile law studyit full mony ane day,

And now my winning is in hevin for ay.

Esope I hecht; my writing and my werk

Is couth and kend to mony cunning clerk."

"O maister Esope, poet lawriate,

God wait ye ar full deir welcum to me.
Ar ye not he that all thir fabillis wrate,
Quhilk in effect, suppois thay fenyeit be,
Ar full off prudence and moralitie?"
"Fair sone," said he, "I am the samin man.
God wait gif that my hert wes merie than.

I said, "Esope, my maister venerabill,
I yow beseik hartlie for cheritie,
Ye wald dedene to tell ane prettie fabill
Concludand with ane gude moralitie."
Schaikand his heid, he said, "My sone, lat be,
For quhat is it worth to tell ane fenyeit taill,
Quhen haly preiching may na thing availl?

"Now in this warld me think richt few or nane
To Goddis word that hes devotioun;
The eir is deif, the hart is hard as stane;
Now oppin sin without correctioun,
The hart inclynand to the eirth ay doun.
Sa roustie is the warld with canker blak
That now my taillis may lytill succour mak."

"Yit, gentill schir," said I, "for my requeist,

Not to displeis your fatherheid, I pray,

Under the figure off ane brutall beist,

Ane morall fabill ye wald denye to say.

Quha wait nor I may leir and beir away

Sum thing thairby heirefter may availl?'

"I grant," quod he, and thus begouth ane taill.

The Fable

Ane lyoun, at his pray wery foirrun,

To recreat his limmis and to rest,

Beikand his breist and belly at the sun,

Under ane tre lay in the fair forest;

Swa come ane trip off myis out off thair nest,

Richt tait and trig, all dansand in ane gyis,

And over the lyoun lansit twyis or thryis.

He lay so still, the myis wes not effeird,

Bot to and fro out over him tuke thair trace;

Sum tirlit at the campis off his beird,

Sum spairit not to claw him on the face;

Merie and glaid, thus dansit thay ane space,

Till at the last the nobill lyoun woke,

And with his pow the maister mous he tuke.

Scho gave ane cry, and all the laif, agast,

Thair dansing left and hid thame sone alquhair.

Scho that wes tane cryit and weipit fast,

And said "Allace" oftymes that scho come thair:

"Now am I tane ane wofull presonair,

And for my gilt traistis incontinent

Off lyfe and deith to thoill the jugement."

Than spak the lyoun to that cairfull mous:

"Thow cative wretche and vile unworthie thing,

Over malapart and eik presumpteous

Thow wes, to mak out over me thy tripping.

Knew thow not weill I wes baith lord and king

Off beistis all?" "Yes," quod the mous, "I knaw,

Bot I misknew, because ye lay so law.

"Lord, I beseik thy kinglie royaltie,

Heir quhat I say, and tak in patience.

Considder first my simple povertie

And syne thy mychtie hie magnyfycence;

Se als how thingis done off neglygence,

Nouther off malice nor of presumtioun,

Erer suld have grace and remissioun.

"We wer repleit and had grit aboundance

Off alkin thingis, sic as to us effeird;

The sweit sesoun provokit us to dance

And mak sic mirth as nature to us leird;

Ye lay so still and law upon the eird

That be my sawll we weind ye had bene deid;

Elles wald we not have dancit over your heid."

"Thy fals excuse," the lyoun said agane,

"Sall not availl ane myte, I underta.

I put the cace, I had bene deid or slane,

And syne my skyn bene stoppit full off stra,

Thocht thow had found my figure lyand swa,

Because it bare the prent off my persoun,

Thow suld for feir on kneis have fallin doun.

"For thy trespas thow can mak na defence,

My nobill persoun thus to vilipend;

Off thy feiris, nor thy awin negligence,

For to excuse thow can na cause pretend;
Thairfoir thow suffer sall ane schamefull end
And deith, sic as to tressoun is decreit,
Onto the gallous harlit be the feit."

"Na, mercie, lord, at thy gentrice I ase,
As thow art king off beistis coronate,
Sober thy wraith, and let it overpas,
And mak thy mynd to mercy inclynate.
I grant offence is done to thyne estate,
Quhairfoir I worthie am to suffer deid,
Bot gif thy kinglie mercie reik remeid.

"In everie juge mercy and reuth suld be
As assessouris and collaterall;
Without mercie, justice is crueltie,
As said is in the lawis spirituall.
Quhen rigour sittis in the tribunall,
The equitie off law quha may sustene?
Richt few or nane, but mercie gang betwene.

"Alswa ye knaw the honour triumphall
Off all victour upon the strenth dependis

Off his conqueist, quhilk manlie in battell
Throw jeopardie of weir lang defendis.
Quhat pryce or loving, quhen the battell endis,
Is said off him that overcummis ane man
Him to defend quhilk nouther may nor can?

"Ane thowsand myis to kill and eik devoir
Is lytill manheid to ane strang lyoun;
Full lytill worschip have ye wyn thairfoir,
To quhais strenth is na comparisoun.
It will degraid sum part off your renoun
To sla ane mous, quhilk may mak na defence
Bot askand mercie at your excellence.

"Also it semis not your celsitude,
Quhilk usis daylie meittis delitious,
To fyle your teith or lippis with my blude,
Quhilk to your stomok is contagious.
Unhailsum meit is of ane sarie mous,
And that namelie untill ane strang lyoun,
Uont till be fed with gentill vennesoun.

"My lyfe is lytill worth, my deith is les,

Yit and I leif I may peradventure
Supple your hienes beand in distres;
For oft is sene, ane man off small stature
Reskewit hes ane lord off hie honour,
Keipit that wes, in poynt to be overthrawin
Throw misfortoun: sic cace may be your awin."

Quhen this wes said, the lyoun his langage
Paissit, and thocht according to ressoun,
And gart mercie his cruell ire asswage,
And to the mous grantit remissioun,
Oppinnit his pow, and scho on kneis fell doun,
And baith hir handis unto the hevin upheild,
Cryand, "Almichty God mot yow foryeild!"

Quhen scho wes gone, the lyoun held to hunt,
For he had nocht, bot levit on his pray,
And slew baith tayme and wyld, as he wes wont,
And in the cuntrie maid ane grit deray;
Till at the last the pepill fand the way
This cruell lyoun how that thay mycht tak.
Off hempyn cordis strang nettis couth thay mak,

And in ane rod, quhair he wes wont to ryn,

With raipis rude fra tre to tre it band;

Syne kest ane range on raw the wod within,

With hornis blast and kennettis fast calland.

The lyoun fled, and throw the ron rynnand

Fell in the net and hankit fute and heid;

For all his strenth he couth mak na remeid,

Welterand about with hiddeous rummissing,

Quhyle to, quhyle fra, quhill he mycht succour get.

Bot all in vane; it vailyeit him na thing;

The mair he flang, the faster wes the net.

The raipis rude wes sa about him plet

On everilk syde, that succour saw he nane,

Bot styll lyand, thus murnand maid his mane.

"O lamit lyoun, liggand heir sa law,

Quhair is the mycht off thy magnyfycence,

Off quhome all brutall beist in eird stude aw,

And dred to luke upon thy excellence?

But hoip or help, but succour or defence,

In bandis strang heir man I ly, allace,

Till I be slane; I se nane uther grace.

"Thair is na wy that will my harmis wreik
Nor creature do confort to my croun.
Quha sall me bute? Quha sall my bandis breik?
Quha sall me put fra pane off this presoun?"
Be he had maid this lamentatioun,
Throw aventure, the lytill mous come neir,
And off the lyoun hard the pietuous beir;

And suddanlie it come in till hir mynd
That it suld be the lyoun did hir grace,
And said, "Now wer I fals and richt unkynd
Bot gif I quit sumpart thy gentilnes
Thow did to me," and on this way scho gais
To hir fellowis, and on thame fast can cry,
"Cum help, cum help!" and thay come all in hy.

"Lo" quod the mous, "this is the samin lyoun
That grantit grace to me quhen I wes tane,
And now is fast heir bundin in presoun,
Brekand his hart with sair murning and mane;
Bot we him help, off souccour wait he nane.
Cum help to quyte ane gude turne for ane uther;
Go, lous him sone"; and thay said, "ye, gude brother."

Thay tuke na knyfe, thair teith wes scharpe anewch;

To se that sicht, forsuith, it wes grit wounder -

How that thay ran amang the rapis tewch,

Befoir, behind, sum yeid abone, sum under,

And schuir the raipis off the net in schunder;

Syne bad him ryse, and he start up anone,

And thankit thame; syne on his way is gone.

Now is the lyoun fre off all danger,

Lows and delyverit to his libertie

Be lytill beistis off ane small power,

As ye have hard, because he had pietie.

Quod I, "Maister, is thair ane moralitie

In this fabill?" "Yea, sone," he said, "richt gude."

"I pray yow, schir," quod I, "Ye wald conclude."

Moralitas

As I suppois, this mychtie gay lyoun

May signifie ane prince or empriour,

Ane potestate, or yit ane king with croun,

Quhilk suld be walkrife gyde and governour

Of his pepill, that takis na labour

To reule and steir the land, and justice keip,
Bot lyis still in lustis, sleuth, and sleip.

The fair forest with levis, lowne and le,
With foulis sang and flouris ferlie sweit,
Is bot the warld and his prosperitie,
As fals plesance, myngit with cair repleit.
Richt as the rois with froist and wynter weit
Faidis, swa dois the warld, and thame desavis
Quhilk in thair lustis maist confidence havis.

Thir lytill myis ar bot the commountie,
Wantoun, unwyse, without correctioun;
Thair lordis and princis quhen that thay se
Of justice mak nane executioun,
Thay dreid na thing to mak rebellioun
And disobey, for quhy thay stand nane aw,
That garris thame thair soveranis misknaw.

Be this fabill, ye lordis of prudence
May considder the vertew pietie,
And to remit sumtyme ane grit offence,
And mitigate with mercy crueltie.

Oftymis is sene ane man of small degré

Hes quit a commoun, baith for gude and ill,

As lord hes done rigour or grace him till.

Quha wait how sone ane lord of grit renoun,

Rolland in wardlie lust and vane plesance,

May be overthrawin, destroyit, and put doun

Throw fals fortoun, quhilk of all variance

Is haill maistres, and leidar of the dance

Till injust men, and blindis thame so soir

That thay na perrell can provyde befoir?

Thir rurall men, that stentit hes the net

In quhilk the lyoun suddandlie wes tane,

Waittit alway amendis for to get,

For hurt men wrytis in the marbill stane.

Mair till expound, as now, I lett allane,

Bot king and lord may weill wit quhat I mene:

Figure heirof oftymis hes bene sene.

Quhen this wes said, quod Esope, "My fair child,

Perswaid the kirkmen ythandly to pray

That tressoun of this cuntrie be exyld,

And justice regne, and lordis keip thair fay

Unto thair soverane king baith nycht and day."

And with that word he vanist and I woke;

Syne throw the schaw my journey hamewart tuke.

The Preaching of the Swallow

The hie prudence and wirking mervelous,

The profound wit off God omnipotent,

Is sa perfyte and sa ingenious,

Excellent far all mannis jugement;

For quhy to Him all thing is ay present,

Rycht as it is or ony tyme sall be,

Befoir the sicht off His divinitie.

Thairfoir our saull with sensualitie

So fetterit is in presoun corporall

We may not cleirlie understand nor se

God as He is, nor thingis celestiall;

Our mirk and deidlie corps materiale

Blindis the spirituall operatioun,

Lyke as ane man wer bundin in presoun.

In Metaphisik Aristotell sayis
That mannis saull is lyke ane bakkis ee,
Quhilk lurkis still, als lang as licht off day is,
And in the gloming cummis furth to fle;
Hir ene ar waik, the sone scho may not se:
Sa is our saull with fantasie opprest,
To knaw the thingis in nature manifest.

For God is in His power infinite,
And mannis saull is febill and over small,
Off understanding waik and unperfite
To comprehend Him that contenis all;
Nane suld presume be ressoun naturall
To seirche the secreitis off the Trinitie,
Bot trow fermelie and lat all ressoun be.

Yit nevertheles we may haif knawlegeing
Off God almychtie be His creatouris,
That He is gude, fair, wyis, and bening.
Exempill tak be thir jolie flouris,
Rycht sweit off smell and plesant off colouris,
Sum grene, sum blew, sum purpour, quhyte, and reid,
Thus distribute be gift off His Godheid.

The firmament payntit with sternis cleir

From eist to west rolland in cirkill round,

And everilk planet in his proper spheir,

In moving makand harmonie and sound;

The fyre, the air, the watter, and the ground -

Till understand it is aneuch, I wis,

That God in all His werkis wittie is.

Luke weill the fische that swimmis in the se;

Luke weill in eirth all kynd off bestyall;

The foulis fair, sa forcelie thay fle,

Scheddand the air with pennis grit and small;

Syne luke to man, that He maid last off all,

Lyke to His image and His similitude:

Be thir we knaw that God is fair and gude.

All creature He maid for the behufe

Off man, and to his supportatioun

In to this eirth, baith under and abufe,

In number, wecht, and dew proportioun;

The difference off tyme, and ilk seasoun

Concorddand till our opurtunitie,

As daylie be experience we may se.

The somer with his jolie mantill grene,

With flouris fair furrit on everilk fent,

Quhilk Flora, goddes off the flouris, quene,

Hes to that lord as for his seasoun lent,

And Phebus, with his goldin bemis gent,

Hes purfellit and payntit plesandly,

With heit and moysture stilland from the sky.

Syne harvest hait, quhen Ceres, that goddes,

Hir barnis benit hes with abundance,

And Bachus, god off wyne, renewit hes

The tume pyipis in Italie and France,

With wynis wicht and liquour off plesance;

And copia temporis to fill hir horne,

That never wes full off quheit nor uther corne.

Syne wynter wan, quhen austerne Eolus,

God off the wynd, with blastis boreall

The grene garment off somer glorious

Hes all to-rent and revin in pecis small.

Than flouris fair faidit with froist man fall,

And birdis blyith changit thair noitis sweit

In styll murning, neir slane with snaw and sleit.

Thir dalis deip with dubbis drounit is,

Baith hill and holt heillit with frostis hair,

And bewis bene ar bethit bair off blis

Be wickit windis off the winter wair.

All wyld beistis than from the bentis bair

Drawis for dreid unto thair dennis deip,

Coucheand for cauld in coifis thame to keip.

Syne cummis ver, quhen winter is away,

The secretar off somer with his sell,

Quhen columbie up keikis throw the clay,

Quhilk fleit wes befoir with froistes fell.

The mavis and the merle beginnis to mell;

The lark on loft, with uther birdis smale,

Than drawis furth fra derne, over doun and daill.

That samin seasoun, in to ane soft morning,

Rycht blyth that bitter blastis wer ago,

Unto the wod, to se the flouris spring,

And heir the mavis sing and birdis mo,

I passit furth, syne lukit to and fro

To se the soill, that wes richt sessonabill,

Sappie, and to resave all seidis abill.

Moving thusgait, grit myrth I tuke in mynd,
Off lauboraris to se the besines,
Sum makand dyke, and sum the pleuch can wynd,
Sum sawand seidis fast frome place to place,
The harrowis hoppand in the saweris trace;
It wes grit joy to him that luifit corne
To se thame laubour, baith at evin and morne.

And as I baid under ane bank full bene,
In hart gritlie rejosit off that sicht,
Unto ane hedge, under ane hawthorne grene,
Off small birdis thair come ane ferlie flicht,
And doun belyif can on the leifis licht
On everilk syde about me quhair I stude,
Rycht mervellous, ane mekill multitude.

Amang the quhilks, ane swallow loud couth cry,
On that hawthorne hie in the croip sittand:
"O ye birdis on bewis heir me by,
Ye sall weill knaw and wyislie understand:
Quhair danger is, or perrell appeirand,
It is grit wisedome to provyde befoir
It to devoyd, for dreid it hurt yow moir."

"Schir Swallow," quod the lark agane, and leuch,
"Quhat have ye sene that causis yow to dreid?"
"Se ye yone churll," quod scho, "beyond yone pleuch
Fast sawand hemp - lo se! - and linget seid?
Yone lint will grow in lytill tyme in deid,
And thairoff will yone churll his nettis mak,
Under the quhilk he thinkis us to tak.

"Thairfoir I reid we pas quhen he is gone
At evin, and with our naillis scharp and small
Out off the eirth scraip we yone seid anone
And eit it up, for giff it growis we sall
Have cause to weip heirefter ane and all.
Se we remeid thairfoir furth-with, instante,
Nam levius laedit quicquid praevidimus ante.

"For clerkis sayis it is nocht sufficient
To considder that is befoir thyne ee;
Bot prudence is ane inwart argument
That garris ane man provyde befoir and se
Quhat gude, quhat evill, is liklie for to be
Off everilk thing evin at the fynall end,
And swa fra perrell ethar him defend."

The lark, lauchand, the swallow thus couth scorne,

And said scho fischit lang befoir the net -

"The barne is eith to busk that is unborne;

All growis nocht that in the ground is set;

The nek to stoup quhen it the straik sall get

Is sone aneuch; deith on the fayest fall."

Thus scornit thay the swallow ane and all.

Despysing thus hir helthsum document,

The foulis ferlie tuke thair flicht anone:

Sum with ane bir thay braidit over the bent,

And sum agane ar to the grene wod gone.

Upon the land quhair I wes left allone

I tuke my club, and hamewart couth I carie,

Swa ferliand as I had sene ane farie.

Thus passit furth quhill June, that jolie tyde,

And seidis that wer sawin off beforne

Wer growin hie, that hairis mycht thame hyde,

And als the quailye craikand in the corne.

I movit furth betuix midday and morne

Unto the hedge under the hawthorne grene,

Quhair I befoir the said birdis had sene,

  And as I stude, be aventure and cace,

The samin birdis as I haif said yow air -

I hoip because it wes thair hanting place,

Mair off succour, or yit mair solitair -

Thay lychtit doun, and quhen thay lychtit wair,

The swallow swyth put furth ane pietuous pyme,

Said, "Wo is him can not bewar in tyme!

"O blind birdis, and full off negligence,

Unmyndfull off your awin prosperitie,

Lift up your sicht and tak gude advertence,

Luke to the lint that growis on yone le!

Yone is the thing I bad, forsuith, that we,

Quhill it wes seid, suld rute furth off the eird:

Now is it lint; now is it hie on breird.

"Go yit, quhill it is tender, young, and small,

And pull it up, let it na mair incres!

My flesche growis, my bodie quaikis all,

Thinkand on it I may not sleip in peis!"

Thay cryit all, and bad the swallow ceis,

And said, "yone lint heirefter will do gude,

For linget is to lytill birdis fude.

"We think, quhen that yone lint bollis ar ryip,

To mak us feist and fill us off the seid,

Magré yone churll, and on it sing and pyip."

"Weill," quod the swallow, "freindes, hardilie beid;

Do as ye will, bot certane, sair I dreid

Heirefter ye sall find als sour as sweit,

Quhen ye ar speldit on yone carlis speit.

"The awner off yone lint ane fouler is,

Richt cautelous and full off subteltie;

His pray full sendill tymis will he mis,

Bot giff we birdis all the warrer be.

Full mony off our kin he hes gart de,

And thocht it bot ane sport to spill thair blude.

God keip me fra him, and the halie Rude!"

Thir small birdis, haveand bot lytill thocht

Off perrell that mycht fall be aventure,

The counsell off the swallow set at nocht,

Bot tuke thair flicht and furth togidder fure;

Sum to the wode, sum markit to the mure.

I tuke my staff, quhen this wes said and done,

And walkit hame, for it drew neir the none.

The lynt ryipit, the carll pullit the lyne,
Rippillit the bollis, and in beitis set,
It steipit in the burne, and dryit syne,
And with ane bittill knokkit it and bet,
Syne swingillit it weill, and hekkillit in the flet;
His wyfe it span, and twynit it in to threid,
Off quhilk the fowlar nettis maid indeid.

The wynter come, the wickit wind can blaw,
The woddis grene wer wallowit with the weit,
Baith firth and fell with froistys wer maid faw,
Slonkis and slaik maid slidderie with the sleit;
The foulis fair, for falt thay fell off feit -
On bewis bair it wes na bute to byde,
Bot hyit unto housis thame to hyde.

Sum in the barn, sum in the stak off corne
Thair lugeing tuke and maid thair residence.
The fowlar saw, and grit aithis hes sworne,
Thay suld be tane trewlie for thair expence;
His nettis hes he set with diligence,
And in the snaw he schulit hes ane plane,
And heillit it all over with calf agane.

Thir small birdis, seand the calff, wes glaid;

Trowand it had bene corne thay lychtit doun,

Bot of the nettis na presume thay had,

Nor of the fowlaris fals intentioun;

To scraip and seik thair meit thay maid thame boun.

The swallow on ane lytill branche neir by,

Dreiddand for gyle, thus loud on thame couth cry:

"Into that calf scraip quhill your naillis bleid –

Thair is na corne, ye laubour all in vane.

Trow ye yone churll for pietie will yow feid?

Na, na, he hes it heir layit for ane trane.

Remove, I reid, or ellis ye will be slane;

His nettis he hes set full prively,

Reddie to draw; in tyme be war for thy!

"Grit fule is he that puttis in dangeir

His lyfe, his honour, for ane thing off nocht.

Grit fule is he that will not glaidlie heir

Counsall in tyme, quhill it availl him mocht.

Grit fule is he that hes na thing in thocht

Bot thing present, and efter quhat may fall

Nor off the end hes na memoriall."

Thir small birdis, for hunger famischit neir,
Full besie scraipand for to seik thair fude,
The counsall off the swallow wald not heir,
Suppois thair laubour dyd thame lytill gude.
Quhen scho thair fulische hartis understude
Sa indurate, up in ane tre scho flew -
With that this churll over thame his nettis drew.

Allace, it wes grit hart sair for to se
That bludie bowcheour beit thay birdis doun,
And for till heir, quhen thay wist weill to de,
Thair cairfull sang and lamentatioun.
Sum with ane staf he straik to eirth on swoun,
Off sum the heid, off sum he brak the crag,
Sum half on lyfe he stoppit in his bag.

And quhen the swallow saw that thay wer deid,
"Lo," quod scho, "thus it happinnis mony syis
On thame that will not tak counsall nor reid
Off prudent men or clerkis that ar wyis.
This grit perrell I tauld thame mair than thryis;
Now ar thay deid, and wo is me thairfoir!"

Scho tuke hir flicht, bot I hir saw no moir.

Moralitas

Lo, worthie folk, Esope, that nobill clerk,

Ane poet worthie to be lawreate,

Quhen that he waikit from mair autentik werk,

With uther ma, this foirsaid fabill wrate,

Quhilk at this tyme may weill be applicate

To gude morall edificatioun,

Haifand ane sentence according to ressoun.

This carll and bond, of gentrice spoliate,

Sawand this calf, thir small birdis to sla,

It is the feind, quhilk fra the angelike state

Exylit is, as fals apostata,

Quhilk day and nycht weryis not for to ga,

Sawand poysoun and mony wickit thocht

In mannis saull, quhilk Christ full deir hes bocht.

And quhen the saull, as seid in to the eird,

Gevis consent in delectatioun,

The wickit thocht beginnis for to breird

In deidlie sin, quhilk is dampnatioun;
Ressoun is blindit with affectioun,
And carnall lust grouis full grene and gay,
Throw consuetude hantit from day to day.

Proceding furth be use and consuetude,
The sin ryipis, and schame is set on syde;
The feynd plettis his nettis scharp and rude,
And under plesance previlie dois hyde;
Syne on the feild he sawis calf full wyde,
Quhilk is bot tume and verray vanitie
Of fleschlie lust and vaine prosperitie.

Thir hungrie birdis, wretchis we may call,
Ay scraipand in this warldis vane plesance,
Greddie to gadder gudis temporall,
Quhilk as the calf ar tume without substance,
Lytill of availl and full of variance,
Lyke to the mow befoir the face of wind
Quhiskis away and makis wretchis blind.

This swallow, quhilk eschaipit is the snair,
The halie preichour weill may signifie,

Exhortand folk to walk, and ay be wair

Fra nettis of our wickit enemie,

Quha sleipis not, bot ever is reddie,

Quhen wretchis in this warldis calf dois scraip,

To draw his net, that thay may not eschaip.

Allace, quhat cair, quhat weiping is and wo,

Quhen saull and bodie partit ar in twane!

The bodie to the wormis keitching go,

The saull to fyre, to everlestand pane.

Quhat helpis than this calf, thir gudis vane,

Quhen thow art put in Luceferis bag,

And brocht to hell, and hangit be the crag?

Thir hid nettis for to persave and se,

This sarie calf wyislie to understand,

Best is bewar in maist prosperitie;

For in this warld thair is na thing lestand;

Is na man wait how lang his stait will stand,

His lyfe will lest, nor how that he sall end

Efter his deith, nor quhidder he sall wend.

Pray we thairfoir quhill we ar in this lyfe

For four thingis: the first, fra sin remufe;

The secund is to seis all weir and stryfe;

The thrid is perfite cheritie and lufe;

The feird thing is, and maist for our behufe,

That is in blis with angellis to be fallow.

And thus endis the preiching of the swallow.

The Fox, the Wolf, and the Cadger

Qwhylum thair wynnit in ane wildernes,

As myne authour expreslie can declair,

Ane revand wolff, that levit upon purches

On bestiall, and maid him weill to fair;

Wes nane sa big about him he wald spair

And he war hungrie, outher for favour or feid,

Bot in his breith he weryit thame to deid.

Swa happinnit him in watching as he went

To meit ane foxe in middis off the way.

He him foirsaw, and fenyeit to be schent,

And with ane bek he bad the wolff gude day.

"Welcum to me," quod he, "thow Russell gray."

Syne loutit doun, and tuke him be the hand:

"Ryse up, Lowrence! I leif the for to stand.

"Quhair hes thow bene this sesoun fra my sicht?

Thow sall beir office, and my stewart be,

For thow can knap doun caponis on the nicht,

And lourand law thow can gar hennis de."

"Schir," said the foxe, "that ganis not for me;

And I am rad, gif thay me se on far,

That at my figure beist and bird will skar."

"Na," quod the wolff, "thow can in covert creip

Upon thy wame and hint thame be the heid,

And mak ane suddand schow upon ane scheip,

Syne with thy wappinnis wirrie him to deid."

"Schir," said the foxe, "ye knaw my roib is reid,

And thairfoir thair will na beist abyde me,

Thocht I wald be sa fals as for to hyde me."

"Yis," quod the wolff, "throw buskis and throw brais

Law can thow lour to come to thy intent."

"Schir," said the foxe, "ye wait weill how it gais;

Ane lang space fra thame thay will feill my sent;

Than will thay eschaip, suppois thay suld be schent;

And I am schamefull for to cum behind thame,

In to the feild thocht I suld sleipand find thame."

"Na," quod the wolff, "thow can cum on the wind;

For everie wrink, forsuith, thow hes ane wyle."

"Schir," said the foxe, "that beist ye mycht call blind

That micht not eschaip than fra me ane myle:

How micht I ane off thame that wyis begyle?

My tippit twa eiris and my twa gray ene

Garris me be kend quhair I wes never sene."

Than said the wolff, "Lowrence, I heir the le,

And castys for perrellis thy ginnes to defend;

Bot all thy sonyeis sall not availl the,

About the busk with wayis thocht thow wend.

Falset will failye ay at the latter end:

To bow at bidding and byde not quhill thow brest,

Thairfoir I giff the counsall for the best."

"Schir," said the foxe, "it is Lentring, ye se;

I can nocht fische, for weiting off my feit,

To tak ane banestikill, thocht we baith suld de;

I have nane uther craft to win my meit.

Bot wer it Pasche, that men suld pultrie eit,

As kiddis, lambis, or caponis in to ply,

To beir your office than wald I not set by."

Than said the wolff in wraith, "Wenis thou with wylis

And with thy mony mowis me to mat?

It is ane auld dog, doutles, that thow begylis;

Thow wenis to drau the stra befoir the cat!"

"Schir," said the foxe, "God wait, I mene not that;

For and I did, it wer weill worth that ye

In ane rude raip had tyit me till ane tre.

"Bot nou I se he is ane fule perfay

That with his maister fallis in ressoning.

I did bot till assay quhat ye wald say;

God wait, my mynd wes on ane uther thing.

I sall fulfill in all thing your bidding,

Quhat ever ye charge on nichtis or on dayis."

"Weill," quod the wolff, "I heir weill quhat thou sayis.

"Bot yit I will thow mak to me ane aith

For to be leill attour all levand leid."

"Schir," said the foxe, "that ane word maks me wraith,
For nou I se ye have me at ane dreid:
Yit sall I sweir, suppois it be not neid,
Be Juppiter, and on pane off my heid,
I sall be treu to you quhill I be deid."

With that ane cadgear, with capill and with creillis,
Come carpand furth; than Lowrence culd him spy.
The foxe the flewer off the fresche hering feillis,
And to the wolff he roundis prively:
"Schir, yone ar hering the cadgear caryis by;
Thairfoir I reid that we se for sum wayis
To get sum fische aganis thir fasting dayis.

"Sen I am stewart, I wald we had sum stuff,
And ye ar silver-seik, I wait richt weill.
Thocht we wald thig yone verray churlische chuff,
He will not giff us ane hering off his creill,
Befoir yone churle on kneis thocht we wald kneill.
Bot yit I trou alsone that ye sall se
Giff I can craft to bleir yone carlis ee.

"Schir, ane thing is, and we get off yone pelff,

Ye man tak travell and mak us sum supple;

For he that will not laubour and help him selff,

In to thir dayis he is not worth ane fle.

I think to work als besie as ane be -

And ye sall follou ane lytill efterwart

And gadder hering, for that sall be your part."

With that he kest ane cumpas far about,

And straucht him doun in middis off the way;

As he wer deid he fenyeit him, but dout,

And than upon lenth unliklie lay.

The quhyte he turnit up off his ene tuay,

His toung out hang ane handbreid off his heid,

And still he lay, als straucht as he wer deid.

The cadgear fand the foxe, and he wes fane,

And till him self thus softlie can he say:

"At the nixt bait, in faith, ye sall be flane,

And off your skyn I sall mak mittenis tway."

He lap full lichtlie about him quhair he lay,

And all the trace he trippit on his tais;

As he had hard ane pyper play he gais.

"Heir lyis the Devyll," quod he, "deid in ane dyke;
Sic ane selcouth sau I not this sevin yeir.
I trou ye have bene tussillit with sum tyke,
That garris you ly sa still withoutin steir.
Schir Foxe, in faith, ye ar deir welcum heir;
It is sum wyfis malisone, I trow,
For pultrie pyking, that lychtit hes on yow.

"Thair sall na pedder, for purs, nor yit for glufis,
Nor yit for poyntis, pyke your pellet fra me:
I sall off it mak mittenis to my lufis
Till hald my handis hait quhair ever I be;
Till Flanderis sall it never saill the se."
With that in hy he hint him be the heillis,
And with ane swak he swang him on the creillis,

Syne be the heid the hors in hy hes hint.
The fraudfull foxe thairto gude tent hes tane,
And with his teith the stoppell, or he stint,
Pullit out, and syne the hering ane and ane
Out off the creillis he swakkit doun gude wane.
The wolff wes war, and gadderit spedilie:
The cadgear sang, "Huntis up, up," upon hie.

Yit at ane burne the cadgear lukit about;

With that the foxe lap quyte the creillis fray.

The cadgear wald have raucht the foxe ane rout,

Bot all for nocht, he wan his hoill that day.

Than with ane schout thus can the cadgear say:

"Abyde, and thou ane nekhering sall haif

Is worth my capill, creillis, and all the laif."

"Now," quod the foxe, "I schreu me and we meit!

I hard quhat thou hecht to do with my skyn.

Thy handis sall never in thay mittinnis tak heit,

And thou wer hangit, carll, and all thy kyn!

Do furth thy mercat - at me thou sall nocht wyn -

And sell thy hering thou hes thair till hie price;

Ellis thow sall wyn nocht on thy merchandice."

The cadgear trimmillit for teyne quhair that he stude.

"It is weill worthie," quod he, "I want yone tyke,

That had nocht in my hand sa mekill gude

As staff or sting yone truker for to stryke."

With that lychtlie he lap out over ane dyke

And hakkit doun ane staff - for he wes tene -

That hevie wes and off the holyne grene.

With that the foxe unto the wolff could wend,
And fand him be the hering quhair he lyis.
"Schir," said he than, "maid I not fair defend?
Ane wicht man wantit never, and he wer wyis;
Ane hardie hart is hard for to suppryis."
Than said the wolff, "Thow art ane berne full bald,
And wyse at will, in gude tyme be it tald.

"Bot quhat wes yone the carll cryit on hie,
And schuke his hand?" quod he. "Hes thou no feill?"
"Schir," said the foxe, "that I can tell trewlie:
He said the nekhering wes in till the creill."
"Kennis thou that hering?" "Ye, schir, I ken it weill,
And at the creill mouth I had it thryis but dout:
The wecht off it neir tit my tuskis out.

"Now suithlie, schir, micht we that hering fang,
It wald be fische to us thir fourtie dayis."
Than said the wolff, "Nou God nor that I hang!
Bot to be thair I wald gif all my clays,
To se gif that my wappinnis mycht it rais."

"Schir," said the foxe, "God wait, I wischit you oft,

Quhen that my pith micht not beir it on loft.

"It is ane syde off salmond, as it wair,

And callour, pypand lyke ane pertrik ee:

It is worth all the hering ye have thair -

Ye, and we had it swa, is it worth sic thre."

Than said the wolff, "Quhat counsell gevis thou me?"

"Schir," said the foxe, "wirk efter my devyis,

And ye sall have it, and tak you na suppryis.

"First, ye man cast ane cumpas far about,

Syne straucht you doun in middis off the way;

Baith heid and feit and taill ye man streik out,

Hing furth your toung, and clois weill your ene tway

Syne se your heid on ane hard place ye lay;

And dout not for na perrell may appeir,

Bot hald you clois, quhen that carll cummis neir.

"And thocht ye se ane staf, have ye na dout,

Bot hald you wonder still in to that steid,

And luke your ene be clois, as thay wer out,

And se that ye schrink nouther fute nor heid:

Than will the cadgear carll trou ye be deid,
And in till haist will hint you be the heillis,
As he did me, and swak you on his creillis."

"Now," quod the wolff, "I sweir the be my thrift,
I trou yone cadgear carll dow not me beir."
"Schir," said the foxe, "on loft he will you lift
Upon his creillis, and do him lytill deir -
Bot ane thing dar I suithlie to you sweir:
Get ye that hering sicker in sum place,
Ye sall not fair in fisching mair quhill Pasche.

"I sall say In principio upon yow,
And crose your corps from the top to tay;
Wend quhen ye will, I dar be warrand now
That ye sall de na suddand deith this day."
With that the wolff gird up sone and to gay,
And caist ane cumpas about the cadgear far;
Syne raucht him in the gait, or he come nar.

He laid his halfheid sicker hard and sad,
Syne straucht his four feit fra him, and his heid,
And hang his toung furth as the foxe him bad;

Als styll he lay as he wer verray deid,

Rakkand na thing off the carlis favour nor feid,

Bot ever upon the nekhering he thinkis,

And quyte foryettis the foxe and all his wrinkis.

With that the cadgear, als wraith as ony wind,

Come rydand on the laid, for it wes licht,

Thinkand ay on the foxe that wes behind,

Upon quhat wyse revenge him best he micht;

And at the last of the wolff gat ane sicht,

Quhair he in lenth lay streikit in the gait -

Bot giff he lichtit doun or nocht, God wait!

Softlie he said, "I wes begylit anis;

Be I begylit twyis, I schrew us baith!

That evill bot it sall licht upon thy banis

He suld have had, that hes done me the skaith."

On hicht he hovit the staf, for he wes wraith,

And hit him with sic will upon the heid

Quhill neir he swonit and swelt in to that steid.

Thre battis he bure, or he his feit micht find,

Bot yit the wolff wes wicht, and wan away;

He mycht not se, he wes sa verray blind,

Nor wit reddilie quhether it wes nicht or day.

The foxe beheld that service quhair he lay,

And leuch on loft quhen he the wolff sa seis,

Baith deif and dosinnit, fall swonand on his kneis.

He that of ressoun can not be content,

Bot covetis all, is abill all to tyne.

The foxe, quhen that he saw the wolff wes schent,

Said to him self, "Thir hering sall be myne."

I le, or ellis he wes efterwart fyne,

That fand sic wayis his maister for to greif.

With all the fische thus Lowrence tuke his leif.

The wolff wes neir weill dungin to the deid,

That uneith with his lyfe away he wan,

For with the bastoun weill brokin wes his heid.

The foxe in to his den sone drew him than,

That had betraisit his maister and the man:

The ane wantit the hering off his creillis;

The utheris blude wes rynnand over his heillis.

Moralitas

This taill is myngit with moralitie,

As I sall schaw sumquhat, or that I ceis.

The foxe unto the warld may likkinnit be;

The revand wolf unto ane man, but leis;

The cadgear, deith, quhome under all man preis -

That ever tuke lyfe throw cours of kynd man dee,

As man, and beist, and fische in to the see.

The warld, ye wait, is stewart to the man,

Quhilk makis man to haif na mynd of deid,

Bot settis for winning all the craftis thay can.

The hering I likkin unto the gold sa reid,

Quhilk gart the wolf in perrell put his heid;

Richt swa the gold garris landis and cieteis

With weir be waistit daylie, as men seis.

And as the foxe with dissimulance and gyle

Gart the wolf wene to haif worschip for ever,

Richt swa this warld with vane glore for ane quhyle

Flatteris with folk, as thay suld failye never;

Yit suddandlie men seis it oft dissever

With thame that trowis oft to fill the sek -

Deith cummis behind and nippis thame be the nek.

The micht of gold makis mony men sa blind,

That settis on avarice thair felicitie,

That thay foryet the cadgear cummis behind

To stryke thame, of quhat stait sa ever thay be:

Quhat is mair dirk than blind prosperitie?

Quhairfoir I counsell mychtie men to haif mynd

Of the nekhering, interpreit in this kynd.

The Fox, the Wolf, and the Husbandman

In elderis dayis, as Esope can declair,

Thair wes ane husband quhilk had ane plewch to steir.

His use wes ay in morning to ryse air:

Sa happinnit him, in streiking tyme off yeir,

Airlie in the morning to follou furth his feir

Unto the pleuch, bot his gadman and he.

His stottis he straucht with "Benedicité!"

The caller cryit, "How! Haik!" upon hicht,

"Hald draucht, my dowis," syne broddit thame full sair:
The oxin wes unusit, young, and licht,
And for fersnes thay couth the fur forfair.
The husband than woxe angrie as ane hair,
Syne cryit, and caist his patill and grit stanis:
"The wolff," quod he, "mot have you all at anis!"

Bot yit the wolff wes neirar nor he wend,
For in ane busk he lay, and Lowrence baith,
In ane rouch rone wes at the furris end,
And hard the hecht; than Lowrence leuch full raith:
"To tak yone bud," quod he, "it wer na skaith."
"Weill," quod the wolff, "I hecht the, be my hand,
Yone carlis word as he wer king sall stand."

The oxin waxit mair reulie at the last;
Syne efter thay lousit, fra that it worthit weill lait;
The husband hamewart with his cattell past.
Than sone the wolff come hirpilland in his gait
Befoir the oxin, and schupe to mak debait.
The husband saw him, and worthit sumdeill agast,
And bakwart with his beistis wald haif past.

The wolff said, "Quhether dryvis thou this pray?
I chalenge it, for nane off thame ar thyne!"
The man thairoff wes in ane felloun fray,
And soberlie to the wolff answerit syne:
"Schir, be my saull, thir oxin ar all myne:
Thairfoir I studdie quhy ye suld stop me,
Sen that I faltit never to you, trewlie."

The wolff said, "Carll, gaif thou not me this drift
Airlie, quhen thou wes eirrand on yone bank?
And is thair oucht, sayis thou, frear than gift?
This tarying wyll tyne the all thy thank:
Far better is frelie for to giff ane plank
Nor be compellit on force to giff ane mart.
Fy on the fredome that cummis not with hart!"

"Schir," quod the husband, "ane man may say in greif,
And syne ganesay fra he avise and se.
I hecht to steill, am I thairfoir ane theif?
God forbid, schir, all hechtis suld haldin be.
Gaif I my hand or oblissing," quod he,
"Or have ye witnes or writ for to schau?
Schir, reif me not, bot go and seik the lau."

"Carll," quod the wolff, "ane lord, and he be leill,

That schrinkis for schame, or doutis to be repruvit -

His sau is ay als sickker as his seill.

Fy on the leid that is not leill and lufit!

Thy argument is fals, and eik contrufit,

For it is said in proverb: "But lawte

All uther vertewis ar nocht worth ane fle."

"Schir," said the husband, "remember of this thing:

Ane leill man is not tane at halff ane taill.

I may say and ganesay; I am na king.

Quhair is your witnes that hard I hecht thame haill?"

Than said the wolff, "Thairfoir it sall nocht faill.

Lowrence," quod he, "cum hidder of that schaw,

And say na thing bot as thow hard and saw."

Lowrence come lourand, for he lufit never licht,

And sone appeirit befoir thame in that place:

The man leuch na thing quhen he saw that sicht.

"Lowrence," quod the wolff, "thow man declair this cace,

Quhairof we sall schaw the suith in schort space.

I callit on the leill witnes for to beir:

Quhat hard thou that this man hecht me lang eir?"

"Schir," said the tod, "I can not hastelie
Swa sone as now gif sentence finall;
Bot wald ye baith submit yow heir to me,
To stand at my decreit perpetuall,
To pleis baith I suld preif, gif it may fall."
"Weill," quod the wolff, "I am content for me."
The man said, "Swa am I, how ever it be."

Than schew thay furth thair allegeance but fabill,
And baith proponit thair pley to him compleit.
Quod Lowrence, "Now I am juge amycabill:
Ye sall be sworne to stand at my decreit,
Quhether heirefter ye think it soure or sweit."
The wolff braid furth his fute, the man his hand,
And on the toddis taill sworne thay ar to stand.

Than tuke the tod the man furth till ane syde,
And said him, "Freind, thou art in blunder brocht;
The wolff will not forgif the ane oxe hyde.
Yit wald my self fane help the, and I mocht,
Bot I am laith to hurt my conscience ocht.
Tyne nocht thy querrell in thy awin defence;

This will not throu but grit coist and expence.

"Seis thou not buddis beiris bernis throw,
And giftis garris crukit materis hald full evin?
Sumtymis ane hen haldis ane man in ane kow;
All ar not halie that heifis thair handis to hevin."
"Schir," said the man, "ye sall have sex or sevin
Richt off the fattest hennis off all the floik -
I compt not all the laif, leif me the coik."

"I am ane juge," quod Lowrence than, and leuch:
"Thair is na buddis suld beir me by the rycht.
I may tak hennis and caponis weill aneuch,
For God is gane to sleip, as for this nycht;
Sic small thingis ar not sene in to His sicht.
Thir hennis," quod he, "sall mak thy querrell sure:
With emptie hand na man suld halkis lure."

Concordit thus, than Lowrence tuke his leiff,
And to the wolff he went in to ane ling;
Syne prevelie he plukkit him be the sleiff:
"Is this in ernist," quod he, "ye ask sic thing?
Na, be my saull, I trow it be in heithing."

Than said the wolff, "Lowrence, quhy sayis thou sa?
Thow hard the hecht thy selff that he couth ma.

"The hecht," quod he, "yone man maid at the pleuch -
Is that the cause quhy ye the cattell craif?"
Halff in to heithing said Lowrence than, and leuch:
"Schir, be the Rude, unroikit now ye raif:
The Devill ane stirk taill thairfoir sall ye haif!
Wald I tak it upon my conscience
To do sa pure ane man as yone offence?

"Yit haif I commonnit with the carll," quod he.
"We ar concordit upon this cunnand:
Quyte off all clamis, swa ye will mak him fre,
Ye sall ane cabok have in to your hand
That sic ane sall not be in all this land,
For it is somer cheis, baith fresche and fair:
He sayis it weyis ane stane and sumdeill mair."

"Is that thy counsell," quod the wolff, "I do,
That yone carll for ane cabok suld be fre?"
"Ye, be my saull, and I wer sworne yow to,
Ye suld nane uther counsell have for me;

For gang ye to the maist extremitie,

It will not wyn yow worth ane widderit neip:

Schir, trow ye not I have ane saull to keip?"

"Weill," quod the wolff, "it is aganis my will

That yone carll for ane cabok suld ga quyte."

"Schir," quod the tod, "ye tak it in nane evill,

For, be my saull, your self had all the wyte."

Than said the wolff, "I bid na mair to flyte,

Bot I wald se yone cabok off sic pryis."

"Schir," said the tod, "he tauld me quhair it lyis."

Than hand in hand thay held unto ane hill;

The husband till his hous hes tane the way,

For he wes fane he schaippit from thair ill,

And on his feit woke the dure quhill day.

Now will we turne unto the uther tway:

Throw woddis waist thir freikis on fute can fair,

Fra busk to busk, quhill neir midnycht and mair.

Lowrence wes ever remembring upon wrinkis

And subtelteis, the wolff for to begyle;

That he had hecht ane caboik he forthinkis;

Yit at the last he findis furth ane wyle,

Than at him selff softlie couth he smyle.

The wolff sayis, "Lowrence, thou playis bellie blind;

We seik all nycht, bot na thing can we find."

"Schir," said the tod, "we ar at it almaist;

Soft yow ane lytill, and ye sall se it sone."

Than to ane manure place thay hyit in haist;

The nycht wes lycht, and pennyfull the mone.

Than till ane draw well thir senyeours past but hone,

Quhair that twa bukkettis severall suithlie hang;

As ane come up ane uther doun wald gang.

The schadow off the mone schone in the well:

"Schir," said Lowrence, "anis ye sall find me leill;

Now se ye not the caboik weill your sell,

Quhyte as ane neip and round als as ane seill?

He hang it yonder that na man suld it steill.

Schir, traist ye weill, yone caboik ye se hing

Micht be ane present to ony lord or king."

"Na," quod the wolff, "mycht I yone caboik haif

On the dry land, as I it yonder se,

I wald quitclame the carll off all the laif:

His dart oxin I compt thame not ane fle;

Yone wer mair meit for sic ane man as me.

Lowrence," quod he, "leip in the bukket sone,

And I sall hald the ane, quhill thow have done."

Lowrence gird doun baith sone and subtellie;

The uther baid abufe and held the flaill.

"It is sa mekill," quod Lowrence, "it maisteris me:

On all my tais it hes not left ane naill.

Ye man mak help upwart, and it haill:

Leip in the uther bukket haistelie,

And cum sone doun and mak me sum supple!"

 Than lychtlie in the bukket lap the loun;

His wecht but weir the uther end gart ryis:

The tod come hailland up, the wolff yeid doun.

Than angerlie the wolff upon him cryis:

"I cummand thus dounwart, quhy thow upwart hyis?"

"Schir," quod the foxe, "thus fairis it off fortoun:

As ane cummis up, scho quheillis ane uther doun."

Than to the ground sone yeid the wolff in haist;

The tod lap on land, als blyith as ony bell,

And left the wolff in watter to the waist.

Quha haillit him out, I wait not, off the well.

Heir endis the text; thair is na mair to tell.

Yyt men may find ane gude moralitie

In this sentence, thocht it ane fabill be.

Moralitas

This wolf I likkin to ane wickit man

Quhilk dois the pure oppres in everie place,

And pykis at thame all querrellis that he can,

Be rigour, reif, and uther wickitnes.

The foxe, the feind I call into this cais,

Arctand ilk man to ryn unrychteous rinkis,

Thinkand thairthrow to lok him in his linkis.

The husband may be callit ane godlie man

With quhome the feynd falt findes, as clerkis reids,

Besie to tempt him with all wayis that he can.

The hennis ar warkis that fra ferme faith proceidis:

Quhair sic sproutis spreidis, the evill spreit thair not speids,

Bot wendis unto the wickit man agane -

That hes tint his travell is full unfane.

The wodds waist, quhairin wes the wolf wyld,
Ar wickit riches, quhilk all men gaipis to get:
Quha traistis in sic trusterie ar oft begyld,
For mammon may be callit the Devillis net,
Quhilk Sathanas for all sinfull hes set:
With proud plesour quha settis his traist thairin,
But speciall grace, lychtlie can not outwin.

The cabok may be callit covetyce,
Quhilk blomis braid in mony mannis ee:
Wa worth the well of that wickit vyce,
For it is all bot fraud and fantasie,
Dryvand ilk man to leip in the buttrie
That dounwart drawis unto the pane of hell -
Christ keip all Christianis from that wickit well!

The Wolf and the Wether

Qwhylum thair wes, as Esope can report,
Ane scheipheird duelland be ane forrest neir,
Quhilk had ane hound that did him grit comfort:
Full war he wes to walk his fauld, but weir,

That nouther wolff nor wildcat durst appeir,

Nor foxe on feild, nor yit no uther beist,

Bot he thame slew, or chaissit at the leist.

Sa happinnit it (as everilk beist man de),

This hound off suddand seiknes to be deid;

Bot than, God wait, the keipar off the fe

For verray wo woxe wanner nor the weid.

"Allace," quod he, "now se I na remeid

To saif the selie beistis that I keip,

For with the wolff weryit beis all my scheip."

It wald have maid ane mannis hart sair to se

The selie scheiphirdis lamentatioun:

"Now is my darling deid, allace," quod he;

"For now to beg my breid I may be boun,

With pyikstaff and with scrip to fair off toun;

For all the beistis befoir that bandonit bene

Will schute upon my beistis with ire and tene."

With that ane wedder wichtlie wan on fute:

"Maister," quod he, "mak merie and be blyith:

To brek your hart for baill it is na bute;

For ane deid dog ye na cair on yow kyith.

Ga fetche him hither and fla his skyn off swyth;

Syne sew it on me - and luke that it be meit,

Baith heid and crag, bodie, taill, and feit.

"Than will the wolff trow that I am he,

For I sall follow him fast quhar ever he fair.

All haill the cure I tak it upon me

Your scheip to keip at midday, lait, and air:

And he persew, be God, I sall not spair

To follow him as fast as did your doig,

Swa that I warrand ye sall not want ane hoig."

Than said the scheipheird, "This come of ane gude wit:

Thy counsall is baith sicker, leill, and trew;

Quha sayis ane scheip is daft, thay lieit of it."

With that in hy the doggis skyn off he flew,

And on the scheip rycht softlie couth it sew.

Than worth the wedder wantoun off his weid:

Now off the wolff," quod he, "I have na dreid."

In all thingis he counterfait the dog,

For all the nycht he stude, and tuke na sleip,

Swa that weill lang thair wantit not ane hog;

Swa war he wes and walkryfe thame to keip,

That Lowrence durst not luke upon ane scheip -

For and he did, he followit him sa fast

That off his lyfe he maid him all agast.

Was nowther wolff, wildcat, nor yit tod

Durst cum within thay boundis all about,

Bot he wald chase thame baith throw rouch and snod.

Thay bailfull beistis had of thair lyvis sic dout,

For he wes mekill and semit to be stout,

That everilk beist thay dred him as the deid,

Within that woid that nane durst hald thair heid.

Yit happinnit thair ane hungrie wolff to slyde

Out throw his scheip, quhair thay lay on ane le:

"I sall have ane," quod he, "quhat ever betyde,

Thocht I be werryit, for hunger or I de."

With that ane lamb in till his cluke hint he;

The laif start up, for thay wer all agast,

Bot God wait gif the wedder followit fast.

Went never hound mair haistelie fra the hand

Quhen he wes rynnand maist raklie at the ra

Nor went this wedder baith over mois and strand,

And stoppit nouther at bank, busk, nor bra,

Bot followit ay sa ferslie on his fa

With sic ane drift, quhill dust and dirt over-draif him,

And maid ane vow to God that he suld have him.

With that the wolff let out his taill on lenth,

For he wes hungrie and it drew neir the ene,

And schupe him for to ryn with all his strenth;

Fra he the wedder sa neir cummand had sene,

He dred his lyfe, and he overtane had bene.

Thairfoir he spairit nowther busk nor boig,

For weill he kennit the kenenes off the doig.

To mak him lycht, he kest the lamb him fra,

Syne lap over leis and draif throw dub and myre.

"Na," quod the wedder, "in faith we part not swa:

It is not the lamb, bot the, that I desyre;

I sall cum neir, for now I se the tyre."

The wolff ran still quhill ane strand stude behind him,

Bot ay the neirar the uedder he couth bind him.

Sone efter that, he followit him sa neir

Quhill that the wolff for fleidnes fylit the feild,

Syne left the gait and ran throw busk and breir,

And schupe him fra the schawis for to scheild.

He ran restles, for he wist off na beild;

The wedder followit him baith out and in,

Quhill that ane breir busk raif rudelie off the skyn.

The wolff wes wer, and blenkit him behind,

And saw the wedder come thrawand throw the breir,

Syne saw the doggis skyn hingand on his lind.

"Na," quod he, "is this ye, that is sa neir?

Richt now ane hound, and now quhyte as ane freir.

I fled over fer, and I had kennit the cais:

To God I vow that ye sall rew this rais.

"Quhat wes the cause ye gaif me sic ane katche?"

With that in hy he hint him be the horne:

"For all your mowis, ye met anis with your matche,

Suppois ye leuch me all this yeir to scorne.

For quhat enchessoun this doggis skyn have ye borne?"

"Maister," quod he, "bot to have playit with yow;

I yow requyre that ye nane uther trow."

"Is this your bourding in ernist than?" quod he,
"For I am verray effeirit, and on flocht:
Cum bak agane, and I sall let yow se."
Than quhar the gait wes grimmit he him brocht:
"Quhether call ye this fair play or nocht:
To set your maister in sa fell effray,
Quhill he for feiritnes hes fylit up the way?

"Thryis, be my saull, ye gart me schute behind:
Upon my hoichis the senyeis may be sene;
For feiritnes full oft I fylit the wind.
Now is this ye? Na, bot ane hound, I wene!
Me think your teith over schort to be sa kene.
Blissit be the busk that reft yow your array;
Ellis, fleand, bursin had I bene this day."

"Schir," quod the wedder, "suppois I ran in hy,
My mynd wes never to do your persoun ill.
Ane flear gettis ane follower commounly,
In play or ernist, preif quha sa ever will.
Sen I bot playit, be gracious me till,
And I sall gar my freindis blis your banis:
Ane full gude servand will crab his maister anis."

"I have bene oftymis set in grit effray,

Bot, be the Rude, sa rad yit wes I never

As thow hes maid me with thy prettie play:

I schot behind quhen thow overtuke me ever.

Bot sikkerlie now sall we not dissever."

Than be crag-bane smertlie he him tuke,

Or ever he ceissit, and it in schunder schuke.

Moralitas

Esope, that poet, first father of this fabill,

Wrait this parabole, quhilk is convenient,

Because the sentence wes fructuous and agreabill,

In moralitie exemplative prudent;

Quhais problemes bene verray excellent,

Throw similitude of figuris, to this day,

Gevis doctrine to the redaris of it ay.

Heir may thow se that riches of array

Will cause pure men presumpteous for to be;

Thay think thay hald of nane, be thay als gay,

Bot counterfute ane lord in all degré.

Out of thair cais in pryde thay clym sa hie

That thay forbeir thair better in na steid,

Quhill sum man tit thair heillis over thair heid.

Richt swa in service uther sum exceidis,

And thay haif withgang, welth, and cherising,

That thay will lychtlie lordis in thair deidis,

And lukis not to thair blude nor thair offspring.

Bot yit nane wait how lang that reull will ring;

Bot he was wyse that bad his sone considder:

Bewar in welth, for hall benkis ar rycht slidder.

Thairfoir I counsell men of everilk stait

To knaw thame self, and quhome thay suld forbeir,

And fall not with thair better in debait,

Suppois thay be als galland in thair geir:

It settis na servand for to uphald weir,

Nor clym sa hie quhill he fall of the ledder

Bot think upon the wolf and on the wedder.

The Wolf and the Lamb

Ane cruell wolff, richt ravenous and fell,

Upon ane tyme past to ane reveir

Descending from ane rotche unto ane well;

To slaik his thrist, drank of the watter cleir.

Swa upon cace ane selie lamb come neir,

Bot of his fa the wolff na thing he wist,

And in the streme laipit to cule his thrist.

Thus drank thay baith, bot not of ane intent:

The wolfis thocht wes all on wickitnes;

The selie lamb wes meik and innocent:

Upon the rever in ane uther place

Beneth the wolff he drank ane lytill space,

Quhill him thocht gude, presomyng thair nane ill.

The wolff this saw, and rampand come him till,

With girnand teith and angrie austre luke,

Said to the lamb, "Thow cative wretchit thing,

How durst thow be sa bald to fyle this bruke

Quhar I suld drink with thy foull slavering?

It wer almous the for to draw and hing,

That suld presume with thy foull lippis wyle

To glar my drink and this fair watter fyle."

The selie lamb, quaikand for verray dreid,

On kneis fell and said, "Schir, with your leif,
Suppois I dar not say thairoff ye leid,
Bot, be my saull, I wait ye can nocht preif
That I did ony thing that suld yow greif;
Ye wait alswa that your accusatioun
Failyeis fra treuth and contrair is to ressoun.

"Thocht I can nocht, nature will me defend,
And off the deid perfyte experience:
All hevie thing man off the selff discend,
Bot giff sum thing on force mak resistence;
Than may the streme on na way mak ascence
Nor ryn bakwart; I drank beneth yow far:
Ergo, for me your bruke wes never the war.

"Alswa my lippis, sen that I wes ane lam,
Tuitchit na thing that wes contagious,
Bot sowkit milk from pappis off my dam,
Richt naturall, sweit, and als delitious."
"Weill," quod the wolff, "thy language rigorus
Cummis the off kynd; swa thy father before
Held me at bait, baith with boist and schore.

"He wraithit me, and than I culd him warne,
Within ane yeir, and I brukit my heid,
I suld be wrokkin on him or on his barne
For his exorbetant and frawart pleid:
Thow sall doutles for his deidis be deid."
"Schir, it is wrang that for the fatheris gilt
The saikles sone suld punist be or spilt.

"Haiff ye not hard quhat Halie Scripture sayis,
Endytit with the mouth off God almycht?
Off his awin deidis ilk man sall beir the pais,
As pyne for sin, reward for werkis rycht;
For my trespas, quhy suld my sone have plycht?
Quha did the mis, lat him sustene the pane."
"Yaa!" quod the wolff. "Yit pleyis thow agane?

"I let the wit, quhen that the father offendis,
I will cheris nane off his successioun,
And off his barnis I may weill tak amendis
Unto the twentie degré descending doun.
Thy father thocht to mak ane strang poysoun,
And with his mouth into my watter spew."
"Schir," quod the lamb, "thay twa ar nouther trew.

"The law sayis, and ye will understand,
Thair suld na man, for wrang nor violence,
His adversar punis at his awin hand
Without proces off law and evidence;
Quhilk suld have leif to mak lawfull defence,
And thairupon summond peremtourly
For to propone, contrairie, or reply.

"Set me ane lauchfull court; I sall compeir
Befoir the lyoun, lord and leill justice,
And be my hand I oblis me rycht heir
That I sall byde ane unsuspect assyis.
This is the law, this is the instant wyis;
Ye suld pretend thairfoir ane summondis mak
Aganis that day, to gif ressoun and tak."

"Na," quod the wolff, "thou wald intruse ressoun
Quhair wrang and reif suld duell in propertie.
That is ane poynt and part of fals tressoun,
For to gar reuth remane with crueltie.
Be Goddis woundis, fals tratour, thow sall de
For thy trespas, and for thy fatheris als."
With that anone he hint him be the hals.

The selie lamb culd do na thing bot bleit:
Sone wes he hedit; the wolff wald do na grace;
Syne drank his blude and off his flesche can eit
Quhill he wes full; syne went his way on pace.
Off his murther quhat sall we say, allace?
Wes not this reuth, wes not this grit pietie,
To gar this selie lamb but gilt thus de?

Moralitas

The pure pepill, this lamb may signifie,
As maill men, merchandis, and all lauboureris,
Of quhome the lyfe is half ane purgatorie,
To wyn with lautie leving, as efferis.
The wolf betakinnis fals extortioneris
And oppressouris of pure men, as we se,
Be violence, or craft in facultie.

Thre kynd of wolfis in this warld now rings:
The first ar fals perverteris of the lawis,
Quhilk under poleit termis falset mingis,
Lettand that all wer gospell that he schawis;

Bot for ane bud the pure man he overthrawis,

Smoirand the richt, garrand the wrang proceid -

Of sic wolfis hellis fyre sall be thair meid.

O man of law, let be thy subteltie,

With nice gimpis and fraudis intricait,

And think that God in his divinitie

The wrang, the richt, of all thy werkis wait.

For prayer, price, for hie nor law estait,

Of fals querrellis se thow mak na defence:

Hald with the richt, hurt not thy conscience.

Ane uther kynd of wolfis ravenous

Ar mychtie men, haifand aneuch plentie,

Quhilkis ar sa gredie and sa covetous

Thay will not thoill in peace ane pureman be:

Suppois he and his houshald baith suld de

For falt of fude, thairof thay gif na rak,

Bot over his heid his mailling will thay tak.

O man but mercie, quhat is in thy thocht?

War than ane wolf, and thow culd understand!

Thow hes aneuch; the pure husband richt nocht,

Bot croip and crufe upon ane clout of land.
For Goddis aw, how durst thow tak on hand -
And thow in barn and byre sa bene and big -
To put him fra his tak and gar him thig?

The thrid wolf ar men of heritage,
As lordis that hes land be Goddis lane,
And settis to the mailleris ane village,
And for ane tyme gressome payit and tane;
Syne vexis him, or half his terme be gane,
With pykit querrellis for to mak him fane
To flit or pay his gressome new agane.

His hors, his meir, he man len to the laird,
To drug and draw in cairt or in cariage;
His servand or his self may not be spaird
To swing and sweit withoutin meit or wage:
Thus how he standis in labour and bondage
That scantlie may he purches by his maill
To leve upon dry breid and watter caill.

Hes thow not reuth to gar thy tennentis sweit
In to thy laubour, with faynt and hungrie wame,

And syne hes lytill gude to drink or eit
With his menye, at evin quhen he cummis hame?
Thow suld be rad for richteous Goddis blame,
For it cryis ane vengeance unto the hevinnis hie
To gar ane pure man wirk but meit or fe.

O thow grit lord, that riches hes and rent,
Be nocht ane wolf, thus to devoir the pure!
Think that na thing cruell nor violent
May in this warld perpetuallie indure.
This sal thow trow and sikkerlie assure:
For till oppres, thow sall haif als grit pane
As thow the pure with thy awin hand had slane.

God keip the lamb, quhilk is the innocent,
From wolfis byit and men extortioneris;
God grant that wrangous men of fals intent
Be manifest, and punischit as effeiris;
And God, as thow all rychteous prayer heiris,
Mot saif our king, and gif him hart and hand
All sic wolfis to banes of the land.

The Paddock and the Mouse

Upon ane tyme, as Esope culd report,
Ane lytill mous come till ane rever syde:
Scho micht not waid, hir schankis wer sa schort;
Scho culd not swym; scho had na hors to ryde;
Off verray force behovit hir to byde;
And to and fra besyde that revir deip
Scho ran, cryand with mony pietuous peip.

"Help over! Help over!" this silie mous can cry,
"For Goddis lufe, sum bodie, over the brym."
With that ane paddok, in the watter by,
Put up hir heid and on the bank can clym,
Quhilk be nature culd douk and gaylie swym.
With voce full rauk, scho said on this maneir:
"Gude morne, schir Mous! Quhat is your erand heir?"

"Seis thow," quod scho, "off corne yone jolie flat,
Off ryip aitis, off barlie, peis, and quheit?
I am hungrie, and fane wald be thair at,
Bot I am stoppit be this watter greit;
And on this syde I get na thing till eit

Bot hard nuttis, quhilkis with my teith I bore:
Wer I beyond, my feist wer fer the more.

"I have no boit; heir is no maryner;
And thocht thair war, I have no fraucht to pay."
Quod scho, "Sister, lat be your hevie cheir;
Do my counsall, and I sall find the way,
Withoutin hors, brig, boit, or yit galay,
To bring yow over saiflie, be not afeird -
And not wetand the campis off thy beird."

"I haif mervell," than quod the lytill mous,
"How can thow fleit without fedder or fin?
This rever is sa deip and dangerous,
Me think that thow suld droun to wed thairin.
Tell me, thairfoir, quhat facultie or gin
Thow hes to bring the over this watter wan."
That to declair the paddok thus began:

"With my twa feit," quod scho, "lukkin and braid,
In steid off airis, I row the streme full styll,
And thocht the brym be perrillous to waid,
Baith to and fra I swyme at my awin will.

I may not droun, for quhy my oppin gill

Devoidis ay the watter I resaiff:

Thairfoir to droun, forsuith, na dreid I haif."

The mous beheld unto hir fronsit face,

Hir runkillit cheikis, and hir lippis syde,

Hir hingand browis, and hir voce sa hace,

Hir loggerand leggis, and hir harsky hyde.

Scho ran abak, and on the paddok cryde:

"Giff I can ony skill off phisnomy,

Thow hes sumpart off falset and invy.

"For clerkis sayis the inclinatioun

Off mannis thocht proceidis commounly

Eter the corporall complexioun

To gude or evill, as nature will apply:

Ane thrawart will, ane thrawin phisnomy.

The auld proverb is witnes off this lorum:

Distortum vultum sequitur distortio morum."

"Na," quod the taid, "that proverb is not trew,

For fair thingis oftymis ar fundin faikin;

The blaberyis, thocht thay be sad off hew,

Ar gadderit up quhen primeros is forsakin;
The face may faill to be the hartis takin;
Thairfoir I find this scripture in all place:
'Thow suld not juge ane man efter his face.'

"Thocht I unhailsum be to luke upon,
I have na wyt quhy suld I lakkit be?
Wer I als fair as jolie Absolon,
I am no causer off that grit beutie;
This difference in forme and qualitie
Almychtie God hes causit dame Nature
To prent and set in everilk creature.

"Off sum the face may be full flurischand,
Off silkin toung and cheir rycht amorous,
With mynd inconstant, fals, and wariand,
Full off desait and menis cautelous."
"Let be thy preiching," quod the hungrie mous,
"And be quhat craft, thow gar me understand,
That thow wald gyde me to yone yonder land."

"Thow wait," quod scho, "ane bodie that hes neid
To help thame self suld mony wayis cast.

Thairfoir ga tak ane doubill twynit threid

And bind thy leg to myne with knottis fast:

I sall the leir to swym - be not agast -

Als weill as I." "As thow?" than quod the mous.

To preif that play, it wer our perrillous!

"Suld I be bund and fast, quhar I am fre,

In hoip off help? Na, than I schrew us baith,

For I mycht lois baith lyfe and libertie!

Giff it wer swa, quha suld amend the skaith,

Bot gif thow sweir to me the murthour aith:

But fraud or gyle to bring me over this flude,

But hurt or harme?" "In faith," quod scho, "I dude."

Scho goikit up, and to the hevin can cry:

"O, Juppiter, off nature god and king,

I mak ane aith trewlie to the, that I

This lytill mous sall over this watter bring."

This aith wes maid; the mous, but persaving

The fals ingyne of this foull carpand pad,

Tuke threid and band hir leg, as scho hir bad.

Than fute for fute thay lap baith in the brym,

Bot in thair myndis thay wer rycht different:
The mous thocht na thing bot to fleit and swym;
The paddok for to droun set hir intent.
Quhen thay in midwart off the streme wer went,
With all hir force the paddok preissit doun,
And thocht the mous without mercie to droun.

Persavand this, the mous on hir can cry:
"Tratour to God, and manesworne unto me!
Thow swore the murthour aith richt now that I
But hurt or harme suld ferryit be and fre."
And quhen scho saw thair wes bot do or de,
Scho bowtit up and forsit hir to swym,
And preissit upon the taiddis bak to clym.

The dreid of deith hir strenthis gart incres,
And forcit hir defend with mycht and mane.
The mous upwart, the paddok doun can pres;
Quhyle to, quhyle fra, quhyle doukit up agane.
This selie mous, plungit in grit pane,
Gan fecht als lang as breith wes in hir breist,
Till at the last scho cryit for ane preist.

Fechtand thusgait, the gled sat on ane twist,

And to this wretchit battell tuke gude heid;

And with ane wisk, or owthir off thame wist,

He claucht his cluke betuix thame in the threid;

Syne to the land he flew with thame gude speid,

Fane off that fang, pyipand with mony pew;

Syne lowsit thame, and baith but pietie slew.

Syne bowellit thame, that boucheour with his bill,

And bellieflaucht full fettislie thame fled,

Bot all thair flesche wald scant be half ane fill,

And guttis als, unto that gredie gled.

Off thair debait, thus quhen I hard outred,

He tuke his flicht and over the feildis flaw.

Giff this be trew, speir ye at thame that saw.

Moralitas

My brother, gif thow will tak advertence,

Be this fabill thow may persave and se

It passis far all kynd of pestilence

Ane wickit mynd with wordis fair and sle.

Be war thairfore with quhome thow fallowis the,

To the wer better beir the stane barrow,

For all thy dayis to delf quhill thow may dre,

Than to be matchit with ane wickit marrow.

Ane fals intent under ane fair pretence

Hes causit mony innocent for to de;

Grit folie is to gif over sone credence

To all that speiks fairlie unto the;

Ane silkin toung, ane hart of crueltie,

Smytis more sore than ony schot of arrow;

Brother, gif thow be wyse, I reid the fle

To matche the with ane thrawart fenyeit marrow.

I warne the als, it is grit nekligence

To bind the fast quhair thow wes frank and fre:

Fra thow be bund, thow may mak na defence

To saif thy lyfe nor yit thy libertie.

This simpill counsall, brother, tak at me,

And it to cun perqueir se thow not tarrow:

Better but stryfe to leif allane in le

Than to be matchit with ane wickit marrow.

This hald in mynd; rycht more I sall the tell

Quhair by thir beistis may be figurate:

The paddok, usand in the flude to duell,

Is mannis bodie, swymand air and lait

In to this warld, with cairis implicate:

Now hie, now law, quhylis plungit up, quhylis doun,

Ay in perrell, and reddie for to droun;

Now dolorus, now blyth as bird on breir;

Now in fredome, now wrappit in distres;

Now haill and sound, now deid and brocht on beir;

Now pure as Job, now rowand in riches;

Now gounis gay, now brats laid in pres;

Now full as fysche, now hungrie as ane hound;

Now on the quheill, now wappit to the ground.

This lytill mous, heir knit thus be the schyn,

The saull of man betakin may in deid -

Bundin, and fra the bodie may not twyn,

Quhill cruell deith cum brek of lyfe the threid -

The quhilk to droun suld ever stand in dreid

Of carnall lust be the suggestioun,

Quhilk drawis ay the saull and druggis doun.

The watter is the warld, ay welterand

With mony wall of tribulatioun,

In quhilk the saull and bodye wer steirrand,

Standand rycht different in thair opinioun:

The saull upwart, the body precis doun;

The saull rycht fane wald be brocht over, I wis,

Out of this warld into the hevinnis blis.

The gled is deith, that cummis suddandlie

As dois ane theif, and cuttis sone the batall.

Be vigilant thairfoir and ay reddie,

For mannis lyfe is brukill and ay mortall.

My freind, thairfoir, mak the ane strang castell

Of gud deidis, for deith will the assay,

Thow wait not quhen - evin, morrow, or midday.

Adew, my freind, and gif that ony speiris

Of this fabill, sa schortlie I conclude,

Say thow, I left the laif unto the freiris,

To mak exempill or similitude.

Now Christ for us that deit on the rude,

Of saull and lyfe as thow art Salviour,

Grant us till pas in till ane blissit hour.

The Testament of Cresseid

Ane doolie sessoun to ane cairfull dyte
Suld correspond and be equivalent:
Richt sa it wes quhen I began to wryte
This tragedie; the wedder richt fervent,
Quhen Aries, in middis of the Lent,
Schouris of haill gart fra the north discend,
That scantlie fra the cauld I micht defend.

Yit nevertheles within myne oratur
I stude, quhen Titan had his bemis bricht
Withdrawin doun and sylit under cure,
And fair Venus, the bewtie of the nicht,
Uprais and set unto the west full richt
Hir goldin face, in oppositioun
Of God Phebus, direct discending doun.

Throwout the glas hir bemis brast sa fair
That I micht se on everie syde me by;
The northin wind had purifyit the air
And sched the mistie cloudis fra the sky;
The froist freisit, the blastis bitterly
Fra Pole Artick come quhisling loud and schill,
And causit me remufe aganis my will.

For I traistit that Venus, luifis quene,

To quhome sum tyme I hecht obedience,
My faidit hart of lufe scho wald mak grene,
And therupon with humbill reverence
I thocht to pray hir hie magnificence;
Bot for greit cald as than I lattit was
And in my chalmer to the fyre can pas.

Thocht lufe be hait, yit in ane man of age
It kendillis nocht sa sone as in youtheid,
Of quhome the blude is flowing in ane rage;
And in the auld the curage doif and deid
Of quhilk the fyre outward is best remeid:
To help be phisike quhair that nature faillit
I am expert, for baith I have assaillit.

I mend the fyre and beikit me about,
Than tuik ane drink, my spreitis to comfort,
And armit me weill fra the cauld thairout.
To cut the winter nicht and mak it schort
I tuik ane quair - and left all uther sport -
Writtin be worthie Chaucer glorious
Of fair Creisseid and worthie Troylus.

And thair I fand, efter that Diomeid
Ressavit had that lady bricht of hew,
How Troilus neir out of wit abraid

And weipit soir with visage paill of hew;
For quhilk wanhope his teiris can renew,
Quhill esperance rejoisit him agane:
Thus quhyle in joy he levit, quhyle in pane.

Of hir behest he had greit comforting,
Traisting to Troy that scho suld mak retour,
Quhilk he desyrit maist of eirdly thing,
For quhy scho was his only paramour.
Bot quhen he saw passit baith day and hour
Of hir ganecome, than sorrow can oppres
His wofull hart in cair and hevines.

Of his distres me neidis nocht reheirs,
For worthie Chauceir in the samin buik,
In gudelie termis and in joly veirs,
Compylit hes his cairis, quha will luik.
To brek my sleip ane uther quair I tuik,
In quhilk I fand the fatall destenie
Of fair Cresseid, that endit wretchitlie.

Quha wait gif all that Chauceir wrait was trew?
Nor I wait nocht gif this narratioun
Be authoreist, or fenyeit of the new
Be sum poeit, throw his inventioun
Maid to report the lamentatioun

And wofull end of this lustie Creisseid,
And quhat distres scho thoillit, and quhat deid.

Quhen Diomeid had all his appetyte,
And mair, fulfillit of this fair ladie,
Upon ane uther he set his haill delyte,
And send to hir ane lybell of repudie
And hir excludit fra his companie.
Than desolait scho walkit up and doun,
And sum men sayis into the court commoun.

O fair Creisseid, the flour and A per se
Of Troy and Grece, how was thow fortunait
To change in filth all thy feminitie,
And be with fleschelie lust sa maculait,
And go amang the Greikis air and lait,
Sa giglotlike takand thy foull plesance!
I have pietie thow suld fall sic mischance!

Yit nevertheles, quhat ever men deme or say
In scornefull langage of thy brukkilnes,
I sall excuse als far furth as I may
Thy womanheid, thy wisdome and fairnes,
The quhilk fortoun hes put to sic distres
As hir pleisit, and nathing throw the gilt
Of the - throw wickit langage to be spilt!

This fair lady, in this wyse destitute

Of all comfort and consolatioun,

Richt privelie, but fellowschip on fute,

Disagysit passit far out of the toun

Ane myle or twa, unto ane mansioun

Beildit full gay, quhair hir father Calchas

Quhilk than amang the Greikis dwelland was.

Quhen he hir saw, the caus he can inquyre

Of hir cumming: scho said, siching full soir,

"Fra Diomeid had gottin his desyre

He wox werie and wald of me no moir."

Quod Calchas, "Douchter, weip thow not thairfoir;

Peraventure all cummis for the best.

Welcum to me; thow art full deir ane gest!"

This auld Calchas, efter the law was tho,

Wes keiper of the tempill as ane preist

In quhilk Venus and hir sone Cupido

War honourit, and his chalmer was neist;

To quhilk Cresseid, with baill aneuch in breist,

Usit to pas, hir prayeris for to say,

Quhill at the last, upon ane solempne day,

As custome was, the pepill far and neir

Befoir the none unto the tempill went
With sacrifice, devoit in thair maneir.
Bot still Cresseid, hevie in hir intent,
Into the kirk wald not hir self present,
For giving of the pepill ony deming
Of hir expuls fra Diomeid the king,

Bot past into ane secreit orature,
Quhair scho micht weip hir wofull desteny.
Behind hir bak scho cloisit fast the dure
And on hir kneis bair fell doun in hy;
Upon Venus and Cupide angerly
Scho cryit out, and said on this same wyse,
"Allace, that ever I maid yow sacrifice!

"Ye gave me anis ane devine responsaill
That I suld be the flour of luif in Troy;
Now am I maid ane unworthie outwaill,
And all in cair translatit is my joy.
Quha sall me gyde? Quha sall me now convoy,
Sen I fra Diomeid and nobill Troylus
Am clene excludit, as abject odious?

"O fals Cupide, is nane to wyte bot thow
And thy mother, of lufe the blind goddes!
Ye causit me alwayis understand and trow

The seid of lufe was sawin in my face,
And ay grew grene throw your supplie and grace.
Bot now, allace, that seid with froist is slane,
And I fra luifferis left, and all forlane."

Quhen this was said, doun in ane extasie,
Ravischit in spreit, intill ane dreame scho fell,
And be apperance hard, quhair scho did ly,
Cupide the king ringand ane silver bell,
Quhilk men micht heir fra hevin unto hell;
At quhais sound befoir Cupide appeiris
The sevin planetis, discending fra thair spheiris;

Quhilk hes power of all thing generabill,
To reull and steir be thair greit influence
Wedder and wind, and coursis variabill:
And first of all Saturne gave his sentence,
Quhilk gave to Cupide litill reverence,
Bot as ane busteous churle on his maneir
Come crabitlie with auster luik and cheir.

His face fronsit, his lyre was lyke the leid,
His teith chatterit and cheverit with the chin,
His ene drowpit, how sonkin in his heid,
Out of his nois the meldrop fast can rin,
With lippis bla and cheikis leine and thin;

The ice schoklis that fra his hair doun hang
Was wonder greit, and as ane speir als lang:

Atouir his belt his lyart lokkis lay
Felterit unfair, ovirfret with froistis hoir,
His garmound and his gyis full of gray,
His widderit weid fra him the wind out woir,
Ane busteous bow within his hand he boir,
Under his girdill ane flasche of felloun flanis
Fedderit with ice and heidit with hailstanis.

Than Juppiter, richt fair and amiabill,
God of the starnis in the firmament
And nureis to all thing generabill;
Fra his father Saturne far different,
With burelie face and browis bricht and brent,
Upon his heid ane garland wonder gay
Of flouris fair, as it had bene in May.

His voice was cleir, as cristall wer his ene,
As goldin wyre sa glitterand was his hair,
His garmound and his gyis full of grene
With goldin listis gilt on everie gair;
Ane burelie brand about his middill bair,
In his richt hand he had ane groundin speir,
Of his father the wraith fra us to weir.

Nixt efter him come Mars the god of ire,
Of strife, debait, and all dissensioun,
To chide and fecht, als feirs as ony fyre,
In hard harnes, hewmound, and habirgeoun,
And on his hanche ane roustie fell fachioun,
And in his hand he had ane roustie sword,
Wrything his face with mony angrie word.

Schaikand his sword, befoir Cupide he come,
With reid visage and grislie glowrand ene,
And at his mouth ane bullar stude of fome,
Lyke to ane bair quhetting his tuskis kene;
Richt tuilyeour lyke, but temperance in tene,
Ane horne he blew with mony bosteous brag,
Quhilk all this warld with weir hes maid to wag.

Than fair Phebus, lanterne and lamp of licht,
Of man and beist, baith frute and flourisching,
Tender nureis, and banischer of nicht;
And of the warld causing, be his moving
And influence, lyfe in all eirdlie thing,
Without comfort of quhome, of force to nocht
Must all ga die that in this warld is wrocht.

As king royall he raid upon his chair,

The quhilk Phaeton gydit sum tyme unricht;
The brichtnes of his face quhen it was bair
Nane micht behald for peirsing of his sicht;
This goldin cart with fyrie bemis bricht
Four yokkit steidis full different of hew
But bait or tyring throw the spheiris drew.

The first was soyr, with mane als reid as rois,
Callit Eoye, into the orient;
The secund steid to name hecht Ethios,
Quhitlie and paill, and sum deill ascendent;
The thrid Peros, richt hait and richt fervent;
The feird was blak, callit Philogié,
Quhilk rollis Phebus doun into the sey.

Venus was thair present, that goddes gay,
Hir sonnis querrell for to defend, and mak
Hir awin complaint, cled in ane nyce array,
The ane half grene, the uther half sabill blak,
With hair as gold kemmit and sched abak;
Bot in hir face semit greit variance,
Quhyles perfyte treuth and quhyles inconstance.

Under smyling scho was dissimulait,
Provocative with blenkis amorous,
And suddanely changit and alterait,

Angrie as ony serpent vennemous,
Richt pungitive with wordis odious;
Thus variant scho was, quha list tak keip:
With ane eye lauch, and with the uther weip,

In taikning that all fleschelie paramour,
Quhilk Venus hes in reull and governance,
Is sum tyme sweit, sum tyme bitter and sour,
Richt unstabill and full of variance,
Mingit with cairfull joy and fals plesance,
Now hait, now cauld, now blyith, now full of wo,
Now grene as leif, now widderit and ago.

With buik in hand than come Mercurius,
Richt eloquent and full of rethorie,
With polite termis and delicious,
With pen and ink to report all reddie,
Setting sangis and singand merilie;
His hude was reid, heklit atovir his croun,
Lyke to ane poeit of the auld fassoun.

Boxis he bair with fyne electuairis,
And sugerit syropis for digestioun,
Spycis belangand to the pothecairis,
With mony hailsum sweit confectioun;
Doctour in phisick, cled in ane skarlot goun,

And furrit weill, as sic ane aucht to be;
Honest and gude, and not ane word culd lie.

Nixt efter him come lady Cynthia,
The last of all and swiftest in hir spheir;
Of colour blak, buskit with hornis twa,
And in the nicht scho listis best appeir;
Haw as the leid, of colour nathing cleir,
For all hir licht scho borrowis at hir brother
Titan, for of hir self scho hes nane uther.

Hir gyse was gray and full of spottis blak,
And on hir breist ane churle paintit full evin
Beirand ane bunche of thornis on his bak,
Quhilk for his thift micht clim na nar the hevin.
Thus quhen thay gadderit war thir goddes sevin,
Mercurius thay cheisit with ane assent
To be foirspeikar in the parliament.

Quha had bene thair and liken for to heir
His facound toung and termis exquisite,
Of rethorick the prettick he micht leir,
In breif sermone ane pregnant sentence wryte.
Befoir Cupide veiling his cap alyte,
Speiris the caus of that vocatioun,
And he anone schew his intentioun.

"Lo," quod Cupide, "quha will blaspheme the name
Of his awin god, outher in word or deid,
To all goddis he dois baith lak and schame,
And suld have bitter panis to his meid.
I say this by yone wretchit Cresseid,
The quhilk throw me was sum tyme flour of lufe,
Me and my mother starklie can reprufe,

"Saying of hir greit infelicitie
I was the caus, and my mother Venus,
Ane blind goddes hir cald that micht not se,
With sclander and defame injurious.
Thus hir leving unclene and lecherous
Scho wald returne in me and my mother,
To quhome I schew my grace abone all uther.

"And sen ye ar all sevin deificait,
Participant of devyne sapience,
This greit injure done to our hie estait
Me think with pane we suld mak recompence;
Was never to goddes done sic violence:
As weill for yow as for my self I say,
Thairfoir ga help to revenge, I yow pray!"

Mercurius to Cupide gave answeir

And said, "Schir King, my counsall is that ye
Refer yow to the hiest planeit heir
And tak to him the lawest of degré,
The pane of Cresseid for to modifie:
As God Saturne, with him tak Cynthia."
"I am content," quod he, "to tak thay twa."

Than thus proceidit Saturne and the Mone
Quhen thay the mater rypelie had degest:
For the dispyte to Cupide scho had done
And to Venus, oppin and manifest,
In all hir lyfe with pane to be opprest,
And torment sair with seiknes incurabill,
And to all lovers be abhominabill.

This duleful sentence Saturne tuik on hand,
And passit doun quhair cairfull Cresseid lay,
And on hir heid he laid ane frostie wand;
Than lawfullie on this wyse can he say,
"Thy greit fairnes and all thy bewtie gay,
Thy wantoun blude, and eik thy goldin hair,
Heir I exclude fra the for evermair.

"I change thy mirth into melancholy,
Quhilk is the mother of all pensivenes;
Thy moisture and thy heit in cald and dry;

Thyne insolence, thy play and wantones,
To greit diseis; thy pomp and thy riches
In mortall neid; and greit penuritie
Thow suffer sall, and as ane beggar die."

O cruell Saturne, fraward and angrie,
Hard is thy dome and to malitious!
On fair Cresseid quhy hes thow na mercie,
Quhilk was sa sweit, gentill and amorous?
Withdraw thy sentence and be gracious -
As thow was never; sa schawis through thy deid,
Ane wraikfull sentence gevin on fair Cresseid.

Than Cynthia, quhen Saturne past away,
Out of hir sait discendit doun belyve,
And red ane bill on Cresseid quhair scho lay,
Contening this sentence diffinityve:
"Fra heit of bodie I the now depryve,
And to thy seiknes sall be na recure
Bot in dolour thy dayis to indure.

"Thy cristall ene mingit with blude I mak,
Thy voice sa cleir unplesand, hoir, and hace,
Thy lustie lyre ovirspred with spottis blak,
And lumpis haw appeirand in thy face:
Quhair thow cummis, ilk man sall fle the place.

This sall thow go begging fra hous to hous
With cop and clapper lyke ane lazarous."

This doolie dreame, this uglye visioun
Brocht to ane end, Cresseid fra it awoik,
And all that court and convocatioun
Vanischit away: than rais scho up and tuik
Ane poleist glas, and hir schaddow culd luik;
And quhen scho saw hir face sa deformait,
Gif scho in hart was wa aneuch, God wait!

Weiping full sair, "Lo, quhat it is," quod sche,
"With fraward langage for to mufe and steir
Our craibit goddis; and sa is sene on me!
My blaspheming now have I bocht full deir;
All eirdlie joy and mirth I set areir.
Allace, this day; allace, this wofull tyde
Quhen I began with my goddis for to chyde!"

Be this was said, ane chyld come fra the hall
To warne Cresseid the supper was reddy;
First knokkit at the dure, and syne culd call,
"Madame, your father biddis yow cum in hy:
He hes merwell sa lang on grouf ye ly,
And sayis your beedes bene to lang sum deill;
The goddis wait all your intent full weill."

Quod scho, "Fair chyld, ga to my father deir
And pray him cum to speik with me anone."
And sa he did, and said, "Douchter, quhat cheir?"
"Allace!" quod scho, "Father, my mirth is gone!"
"How sa?" quod he, and scho can all expone,
As I have tauld, the vengeance and the wraik
For hir trespas Cupide on hir culd tak.

He luikit on hir uglye lipper face,
The quhylk befor was quhite as lillie flour;
Wringand his handis, oftymes he said allace
That he had levit to se that wofull hour;
For he knew weill that thair was na succour
To hir seiknes, and that dowblit his pane;
Thus was thair cair aneuch betuix thame twane.

Quhen thay togidder murnit had full lang,
Quod Cresseid, "Father, I wald not be kend;
Thairfoir in secreit wyse ye let me gang
To yone hospitall at the tounis end,
And thidder sum meit for cheritie me send
To leif upon, for all mirth in this eird
Is fra me gane; sic is my wickit weird!"

Than in ane mantill and ane bawer hat,

With cop and clapper, wonder prively,
He opnit ane secreit get and out thair at
Convoyit hir, that na man suld espy,
Unto ane village half ane myle thairby;
Delyverit hir in at the spittaill hous,
And daylie sent hir part of his almous.

Sum knew hir weill, and sum had na knawledge
Of hir becaus scho was sa deformait,
With bylis blak ovirspred in hir visage,
And hir fair colour faidit and alterait.
Yit thay presumit, for hir hie regrait
And still murning, scho was of nobill kin;
With better will thairfoir they tuik hir in.

The day passit and Phebus went to rest,
The cloudis blak ouerheled all the sky.
God wait gif Cresseid was ane sorrowfull gest,
Seing that uncouth fair and harbery!
But meit or drink scho dressit hir to ly
In ane dark corner of the hous allone,
And on this wyse, weiping, scho maid hir mone.

The Complaint of Cresseid

"O sop of sorrow, sonkin into cair,
O cative Creisseid, for now and ever mair
Gane is thy joy and all thy mirth in eird;
Of all blyithnes now art thou blaiknit bair;
Thair is na salve may saif the of thy sair!
Fell is thy fortoun, wickit is thy weird,
Thy blys is baneist, and thy ball on breird!
Under the eirth, God gif I gravin wer,
Quhair nane of Grece nor yit of Troy micht heird!

"Quhair is thy chalmer wantounlie besene,
With burely bed and bankouris browderit bene;
Spycis and wyne to thy collatioun,
The cowpis all of gold and silver schene,
Thy sweit meitis servit in plaittis clene
With saipheron sals of ane gude sessoun;
Thy gay garmentis with mony gudely goun,
Thy plesand lawn pinnit with goldin prene
All is areir, thy greit royall renoun!

"Quhair is thy garding with thir greissis gay
And fresche flowris, quhilk the quene Floray
Had paintit plesandly in everie pane,
Quhair thou was wont full merilye in May

To walk and tak the dew be it was day,
And heir the merle and mawis mony ane,
With ladyis fair in carrolling to gane
And se the royall rinkis in thair array,
In garmentis gay garnischit on everie grane?

"Thy greit triumphand fame and hie honour,
Quhair thou was callit of eirdlye wichtis flour,
All is decayit, thy weird is welterit so;
Thy hie estait is turnit in darknes dour;
This lipper ludge tak for thy burelie bour,
And for thy bed tak now ane bunche of stro,
For waillit wyne and meitis thou had tho
Tak mowlit breid, peirrie and ceder sour;
Bot cop and clapper now is all ago.

"My cleir voice and courtlie carrolling,
Quhair I was wont with ladyis for to sing,
Is rawk as ruik, full hiddeous, hoir and hace;
My plesand port, all utheris precelling,
Of lustines I was hald maist conding -
Now is deformit the figour of my face;
To luik on it na leid now lyking hes.
Sowpit in syte, I say with sair siching,
Ludgeit amang the lipper leid, `Allace!'

"O ladyis fair of Troy and Grece, attend
My miserie, quhilk nane may comprehend,
My frivoll fortoun, my infelicitie,
My greit mischeif, quhilk na man can amend.
Be war in tyme, approchis neir the end,
And in your mynd ane mirrour mak of me:
As I am now, peradventure that ye
For all your micht may cum to that same end,
Or ellis war, gif ony war may be.

"Nocht is your fairnes bot ane faiding flour,
Nocht is your famous laud and hie honour
Bot wind inflat in uther mennis eiris,
Your roising reid to rotting sall retour;
Exempill mak of me in your memour
Quhilk of sic thingis wofull witnes beiris.
All welth in eird, away as wind it weiris;
Be war thairfoir, approchis neir your hour;
Fortoun is fikkill quhen scho beginnis and steiris."

Thus chydand with hir drerie destenye,
Weiping scho woik the nicht fra end to end;
Bot all in vane; hir dule, hir cairfull cry,
Micht not remeid, nor yit hir murning mend.
Ane lipper lady rais and till hir wend,
And said, "Quhy spurnis thow aganis the wall

To sla thy self and mend nathing at all?

"Sen thy weiping dowbillis bot thy wo,
I counsall the mak vertew of ane neid;
Go leir to clap thy clapper to and fro,
And leif efter the law of lipper leid."
Thair was na buit, bot furth with thame scho yeid
Fra place to place, quhill cauld and hounger sair
Compellit hir to be ane rank beggair.

That samin tyme, of Troy the garnisoun,
Quhilk had to chiftane worthie Troylus,
Throw jeopardie of weir had strikken doun
Knichtis of Grece in number mervellous;
With greit tryumphe and laude victorious
Agane to Troy richt royallie thay raid
The way quhair Cresseid with the lipper baid.

Seing that companie, all with ane stevin
Thay gaif ane cry, and schuik coppis gude speid,
"Worthie lordis, for Goddis lufe of hevin,
To us lipper part of your almous deid!"
Than to thair cry nobill Troylus tuik heid,
Having pietie, neir by the place can pas
Quhair Cresseid sat, not witting quhat scho was.

Than upon him scho kest up baith hir ene,
And with ane blenk it come into his thocht
That he sumtime hir face befoir had sene,
Bot scho was in sic plye he knew hir nocht;
Yit than hir luik into his mynd it brocht
The sweit visage and amorous blenking
Of fair Cresseid, sumtyme his awin darling.

Na wonder was, suppois in mynd that he
Tuik hir figure sa sone, and lo, now quhy:
The idole of ane thing in cace may be
Sa deip imprentit in the fantasy
That it deludis the wittis outwardly,
And sa appeiris in forme and lyke estait
Within the mynd as it was figurait.

Ane spark of lufe than till his hart culd spring
And kendlit all his bodie in ane fyre;
With hait fewir, ane sweit and trimbling
Him tuik, quhill he was reddie to expyre;
To beir his scheild his breist began to tyre;
Within ane quhyle he changit mony hew;
And nevertheles not ane ane uther knew.

For knichtlie pietie and memoriall
Of fair Cresseid, ane gyrdill can he tak,

Ane purs of gold, and mony gay jowall,
And in the skirt of Cresseid doun can swak;
Than raid away and not ane word he spak,
Pensiwe in hart, quhill he come to the toun,
And for greit cair oft syis almaist fell doun.

The lipper folk to Cresseid than can draw
To se the equall distributioun
Of the almous, bot quhen the gold thay saw,
Ilk ane to uther prewelie can roun,
And said, "yone lord hes mair affectioun,
How ever it be, unto yone lazarous
Than to us all; we knaw be his almous."

"Quhat lord is yone," quod scho, "have ye na feill,
Hes done to us so greit humanitie?"
"Yes," quod a lipper man, "I knaw him weill;
Schir Troylus it is, gentill and fre."
Quhen Cresseid understude that it was he,
Stiffer than steill thair stert ane bitter stound
Throwout hir hart, and fell doun to the ground.

Quhen scho ouircome, with siching sair and sad,
With mony cairfull cry and cald ochane:
"Now is my breist with stormie stoundis stad,
Wrappit in wo, ane wretch full will of wane!"

Than fel in swoun full oft or ever scho fane,
And ever in hir swouning cryit scho thus,
"O fals Cresseid and trew knicht Troylus!

"Thy lufe, thy lawtie, and thy gentilnes
I countit small in my prosperitie,
Sa efflated I was in wantones,
And clam upon the fickill quheill sa hie.
All faith and lufe I promissit to the
Was in the self fickill and frivolous:
O fals Cresseid and trew knicht Troilus!

"For lufe of me thow keipt continence,
Honest and chaist in conversatioun;
Of all wemen protectour and defence
Thou was, and helpit thair opinioun;
My mynd in fleschelie foull affectioun
Was inclynit to lustis lecherous:
Fy, fals Cresseid; O trew knicht Troylus!

"Lovers be war and tak gude heid about
Quhome that ye lufe, for quhome ye suffer paine.
I lat yow wit, thair is richt few thairout
Quhome ye may traist to have trew lufe agane;
Preif quhen ye will, your labour is in vaine.
Thairfoir I reid ye tak thame as ye find,

For thay ar sad as widdercok in wind.

"Becaus I knaw the greit unstabilnes,
Brukkill as glas, into my self, I say -
Traisting in uther als greit unfaithfulnes,
Als unconstant, and als untrew of fay -
Thocht sum be trew, I wait richt few ar thay;
Quha findis treuth, lat him his lady ruse;
Nane but my self as now I will accuse."

Quhen this was said, with paper scho sat doun,
And on this maneir maid hir testament:
"Heir I beteiche my corps and carioun
With wormis and with taidis to be rent;
My cop and clapper, and myne ornament,
And all my gold the lipper folk sall have,
Quhen I am deid, to burie me in grave.

"This royall ring, set with this rubie reid,
Quhilk Troylus in drowrie to me send,
To him agane I leif it quhen I am deid,
To mak my cairfull deid unto him kend.
Thus I conclude schortlie and mak ane end:
My spreit I leif to Diane, quhair scho dwellis,
To walk with hir in waist woddis and wellis.

"O Diomeid, thou hes baith broche and belt
Quhilk Troylus gave me in takning
Of his trew lufe," and with that word scho swelt.
And sone ane lipper man tuik of the ring,
Syne buryit hir withouttin tarying;
To Troylus furthwith the ring he bair,
And of Cresseid the deith he can declair.

Quhen he had hard hir greit infirmitie,
Hir legacie and lamentatioun,
And how scho endit in sic povertie,
He swelt for wo and fell doun in ane swoun;
For greit sorrow his hart to brist was boun;
Siching full sadlie, said, "I can no moir;
Scho was untrew and wo is me thairfoir."

Sum said he maid ane tomb of merbell gray,
And wrait hir name and superscriptioun,
And laid it on hir grave quhair that scho lay,
In goldin letteris, conteining this ressoun:
"Lo, fair ladyis, Cresseid of Troy the toun,
Sumtyme countit the flour of womanheid,
Under this stane, lait lipper, lyis deid."

Now, worthie wemen, in this ballet schort,
Maid for your worschip and instructioun,

Of cheritie, I monische and exhort,
Ming not your lufe with fals deceptioun:
Beir in your mynd this schort conclusioun
Of fair Cresseid, as I have said befoir.
Sen scho is deid I speik of hir no moir.

The Laste Epistle of Creseyd to Troyalus

Healthe, healthe to worthy Troylus dothe
His sometyme Cresyed send,
If so she may whose lothed lyfe
And lynes at ones must end.
My wish unseene was but to see
The ones before my deathe,
Which sight unawares yet longe desyred
Dothe stopp my vitall breathe. 1
For destinies hathe me well assured
My rewfull race is ronne,
And Atropos with sythe in hande
Is redye to undone
The fatall threid that Lashesses
And Clotho once did twyne,
And hightes to haste my welcome deathe
And longe desyred fyne.
The cruell goddes to Creaseyda

Unfrindlye foes have beyne,
That would to god some savage beaste
Had me devoured cleane.
When I of Troye was calld a chylde
And Phrigia soyle I sawe,
Would [that] the earthe my little lymms
Into hir wombe had drawe.
Then should no poet have the cause
Faire Creyseydes treuthe to blame,
Nor after this with ladyes falce
Remember Creseydes name;
Ne yet no mann his fickle dame
With Creseyd should upbraid,
Nor by examples bringe me in
Howe Troyolus was betrayde.
But would to god that Hecuba
Had Priamus will fulfilld,
And Paris as the prophetts had
Unlucky ladd had killd;
Or ells that he with Oenon yet
Had taried still in Ide,
And lyke a sheperd fed his flocke
By olde Scamanders syde,
And not for Priams sonne beyne know,
Nor Hectors brother namde.
But O the fates, the froward fates,

Hath thus his fortune framde
That he the swellinge seas should sayle
And Menelaus wyfe
By rape should bringe, & breid tweene Greekes
And Trojans mortall stryfe;
Which in thend, as godes forbidd,
Should tourne in flashye flame
The princely pallace, Illion brave,
Of moste renowme & fame.
O rather wish I that the songe
Of sousinge seas had drencht
The leiches twayne, & all the fyre
Of love by water quencht.
Then should no greater Eageon sandes
With shearing shipp have sought
Mo thousande barged to thy shore,
O Troya towne, have brought.
Then should my father Calcas not
His natyve soyle have fledd,
When he to Tenidos was sent
To seeke Appolloes neid,
And then my haples husband had
Not stand in deadly feilde
In fight amongst the furious Greekes
All armed under sheilde.

Then should myne honour have beyne kept
Myne honestye unfoulde.
But Troyalus thou didst that defend
As well as thester colde:
For thou moste trewe, most pacient was,
Moste secret to thy love,
That ever ladye had ere this,
Or after this may proove.
For 3 yeares space no lyffe but one,
One love that did espye.
But why doe I thus wish & woulde?
I waste but tyme therby.
All thinges that womans prayse should bringe
In me is quyte defyled,
That ought a worthy ladye have
A Grekish kinge hathe spoylde;
That shrouded is the shyninge light
As nyght dothe blisfull daye.
So curse I may the hatefull hower
Yea, well it curse I maye,
That Anthono by chance of warr
And force of Greekes was take,
For whom they me & Thoas sende
A full exchange to make.

Was ther no other pledge, allas,
Or was it me they seike?
Why might not for a Trojayne duke
Suffise a kinge, a Greik?
Nay, mans provision was it not,
It was the deadlye doome
The fates ay from my birthe did threat
Uppon my head should come.
Than out on all these dreyry dames
That destenyes dothe dispyse,
And out on Fortune, fy on hope,
The weaver of my woes.
And nowe you angry nimphes whose plagues
I feile uppon me ryffe,
Your hate from hence can harme me nought
Except ye lengthe me lyfe.
But O my Troylus, if I darr
Usurpe this phrase aright,
Howe could thy knightly harte consent,
Or eyes abyde the sight,
To see me under Diomedes guarde
From Troy to Greikes so stray?
Why slewest thou not thy mortall foe
And fled with me awaye?

No, thou extemed myne honour soe
Myne honestye to blott
Thou was affrayde, or ells thou shouldst
Have done it well I wote.
For thou no sooner tooke thy love
Of me, nor from me went,
When Diomede with his sleated lipps
Hathe faste my bridle hent;
And then he sharpes his subtill will,
And faste his brayne he fyles,
And tipps his tongue with retoricks sweit,
Bewitchinge me with wyles,
And layethe me forthe his love alonge,
He no persuasion spares:
Sometymes he piteous tears dothe shedd,
Some tyme as madd he stayres;
Then dothe he bragg of parentes stout,
And in these eares of myne
He ringes me out his royall race
And tells his stately lyne;
Of Meliagers force he boastes,
And howe the Bore he smightes,
And howe his father Tedeus slewe
Well armed fiftye knightes.
Then dothe he promise golden hills,
Nowe hight me giftes full large;

Forthwith he swears to make me quene

Of Callidon & Arge.

But looke, even as the whiskinge wyndes

Of Borias blasting boulde

Amid the playne & champion feildes

May take no staye or holde,

His talke so one eare fills & out

At t'other streight dothe goe;

For then I was to Troyalus vowed,

I swore to love no moe.

And thus so prates me on the waye,

Till of the Grekish hoste

We had a sight; he seinge then

His mynde in vayne was loste

Did hartely pray, & me intreat,

As humblie as he can,

T'accept him as my servant. Lo,

What should I doe? As then

I tooke him, so his painted wordes

So muche did me abuse.

But Troyalus, O moste worthy knight,

Of the I crave excuse.

Too hastye thou may thinke I was:

I might have yet delayed.

Allas, to hastye may I saye.

What travells longe thou made,

And Pandarus, eare ye could bringe
The halfe of this to passe;
His cursinges weighe me downe to hell:
I feile ther payse, allas.
Nowe, nowe, my witt, wher be your help?
Some apte excuse to make
All wemen can devyse at will,
Yet myne, allas, are slacke.
But what excuse may me availe?
My consience is attaint.
For shame I feile my blood to faile,
My dyenge lymmes are faynte.
And nowe amidd the campe of Greekes
We came, & as we paste,
Myne aged father, glad to se
Me, ledd me in as faste.
Thatredes, wreakfull brethern bothe,
Doe muche my bewtye prayse:
The Lordes of Greece me welcomes bring,
The soldiers on me gaze.
As soone as Phoebus on the moone
From coutche did clymbe the skyes,
Sir Diomede to the tent I lay
With spedy pace him plyes,
And faste he prayes, desyres, intreates
Me him some signe to plight

Wherby he might be knowne my man,
My servant, or my knight;
And kyndenes dothe he on me threape,
As all were his at firste;
But yet he frustrate was as then,
Althoughe his harte should burste.
But then my father tolde me that
I must still ther sojourne,
And me assurd I never shoulde
To Troye againe retourne.
Then caste I in my troubled mynde
That Troyalus I had lorne;
Who sorrowed then but Cresyda
As ta fountaine I shoulde tourne.
No consolacion could I fynde,
And then, considderinge well
Howe I a woman was alone
And dayly fortunes fell,
What happs might chance me I ne knewe,
I studyed this full longe.
My father olde, Sir Troyalus loste,
Then must I beare eche wronge.
Nowe this, nowe that, I ryfle upp
Within my buissy brayne,
Whyles will I with my father staye,
Whyles steale to Troye againe.

A sevenight thus I lived; huge fight
Was dayly still without,
Stronge garde within, eche thinge presentes
Unto my harte a doubte.
I pondringe thus, thou sent the Greik,
Sir Diomeid, to his tent
With woundes profounde & lardge which thou
In irefull rage him lent;
To whom I came, not myndinge evill
But frindely him to veiwe,
And tooke my leave; but he anon
Did fresh his mater shewe,
And me besought in humble wyse
To rewe uppon his smarte.
I, reckles wight, to soone, allas,
Did hight him ther my harte.
Thou demed full lyte of all this fare.
Thou thoght I was none suche
Till that on Diomeds cote of armes
Thou spyed the little bruche.
For after that full oft thou wouldste
With Creseyd him uprayde,
And for my sake, as was me tolde,
Thou haste him sore outrayde.

With thawked armes, & helme to dasht,

With speare full sharpe igrounde,

Scarce curable thou pearst his fleshe

With many a grevous wounde.

Why on this traytour stay I thus?

The goddes me on him wreake.

Let fate worke on: lyfe leaves my limms,

Even scarcely may I speake.

He falsed hathe his faithe to me,

And lightlied me, allas.

Of force the courte I left, & to

My fathers house did passe.

The crewell godes not yet content

With me to make accordd,

My luringe face they leaper made:

To se me, men abhord.

To hospitall by night I stole

My self from sight to save,

Wher me was given a clappinge dishe

My wretched cromms to crave;

As thou me foundst, when as thou caste

Thy golde into my lapp.

Wouldst thou, O Troyalus, thought ther should

Have chaunst me suche mishapp?

Ye famous painters wonted were

To drawe with coulers pure

The forme of thinge, with dainty hande,

For evermore endure;

And ye ingravers, purposely,

Suche artes as erste were paste,

Did beate in massy marble stronge

Eternally to laste.

But love, in mowld of memory,

Imprintes in perfitt harte

The loved, so that deathe itself

Can noght the same devert.

As nowe by the, O Troyalus deare,

I plainely may appeare,

Dothe ought resemble yet the shape

That Cresyade once did beare?

It cannot be; but nowe, but nowe,

My ghost must hence depart.

I feile the stinge of gaspinge deathe

Dothe strayne me by the harte.

No gratefull token may I send,

My golden giftes are scante.

My harte to send thou might refuse

And say it truthe dothe wante.

Except a ringe, nought ells I have,

Which thou me gave that night

That joyned was our hartes in one

And faythe to others plight,

The which I send in paper lapte,

Bewashed with teares,

By him that beares my latest lynes

And funerall that heares.

But this had I almoste forgott,

So troubleth deathe my mynde,

That thou voutchsafe tentere the coirps

That oft thyne armes hathe wynde;

And on my tombe some epitaphe

Engrave as lykes the beste.

So fayre the well: this lipers knight

Can showe of me the rest.

Orpheus and Eurydice

The nobilnes and grit magnificens

Of prince and lord, quhai list to magnifie,

His ancestré and lineall discens

Suld first extoll, and his genolegie,

So that his harte he mycht inclyne thairby

The moir to vertew and to worthiness,

Herand reherss his eldiris gentilness.

It is contrair the lawis of nature

A gentill man to be degenerat,
Noucht following of his progenitour
The worthé rewll and the lordly estait;
A ryall rynk for to be rusticat
Is bot a monsture in comparesoun,
Had in dispyt and foule derisioun.

I say this be the grit lordis of Grew,
Quhilk sett thair hairt and all thair haill curage
Thair faderis steppis justly to persew,
Eiking the wirschep of thair he lenage;
The ancient and sadwyse men of age
War tendouris to yung and insolent
To mak thame in all vertewis excellent.

Lyk as a strand of water or a spring
Haldis the sapour of the fontell well,
So did in Grece ilk lord and worthy king,
Of forebearis thay tuk tarage and smell;
Among the quhilk of ane I think to tell,
Bot first his gentill generatioun
I sall rehers, with youre correctioun.

Upone the mont of Eleconé,
The most famous of all Arrabea,
A goddes dwelt, excellent in bewté,

Gentill of blude, callit Memoria,
Quhilk Jupiter that goddes to wyfe can ta,
And carnaly hir knew, quhilk eftir syne
Apone a day bare him fair dochteris nyne.

The first in Grew wes callit Euterpé,
In our language gude delectatioun;
The secound maid clippit Melpomyné,
As hony sueit in modelation;
Thersycoré is gud instructioun
Of every thing, the thrid sister, I wiss,
Thus out of Grew in Latyne translait is;

Caliopé, that madin mervalouss,
The ferd sistir, of all musik maistress,
And mother to the king, schir Orpheouss,
Quhilk throw his wyfe was efter king of Traiss;
Clio, the fyift, that now is a goddess,
In Latyne callit meditatioun
Of everything that hes creatioun;

The sext sister is callit Herato,
Quhilk drawis lyk to lyk in every thing;
The sevint lady was fair Polimio,
Quhilk cowth a thowsand sangis suietly sing;
Talia syne, quhilk can our saulis bring

To profound wit and grit agilité
Till undirstand and haif capacitie;

Urania, the nynt and last of all,
In Greik langage, quha cowth it rycht expound,
Is callit armony celestiall,
Rejosing men with melody and sound.
Amang thir nyne Calliopé was cround
And maid a quene be michty god Phebuss,
Off quhome he gat this prince, schir Orpheouss.

No wondir wes thocht he wes fair and wyse,
Gentill and gud, full of liberalitie,
His fader god, and his progenetryse
A goddess, finder of all armony.
Quhen he was borne scho set him on hir kne
And gart him souk of hir twa paupis quhyte
The sueit lecour of all musik perfyte.

Incressand sone to manheid up he drew,
Off statur large and frely fair of face;
His noble fame so far it sprang and grew,
Till at the last the michty quene of Trace,
Excelland fair, haboundand in richess,
A message send unto that prince so ying,
Requyrand him to wed hir and be king.

Euridices this lady had to name;
And quhene scho saw this prince so glorius,
Hir erand to propone scho thocht no schame;
With wordis sueit and blenkis amorouss,
Said, "Welcum, lord and lufe, schir Orpheuss:
In this provynce ye sal be king and lord!"
Thai kissit syne, and thus thay can accord.

Betuix Orpheuss and fair Euridices,
Fra thai war weddit on fra day to day,
The low of lufe cowth kyndill and incres,
With mirth and blythnes, solace and with play.
Off wardly joy, allace, quhat sall I say?
Lyk till a flour that plesandly will spring,
Quhilk fadis sone, and endis with murnyng.

I say this be Erudices the quene,
Quhilk walkit furth in to a May mornyng,
Bot with a madyn untill a medow grene,
To tak the air and se the flouris spring;
Quhair in a schaw, neir by this lady ying,
A busteous hird, callit Arresteuss,
Kepand his beistis, lay undir a buss.

And quhen he saw this lady solitar,

Bairfut with schankis quhyter than the snaw,
Preckit with lust, he thocht withoutin mair
Hir till oppress - and till hir can he drawe.
Dreidand for evill, scho fled quhen scho him saw,
And as scho ran all bairfute on a buss,
Scho trampit on a serpent vennemuss.

This crewall venome was so penetrife,
As natur is of all mortall pusoun,
In peisis small this quenis harte can rife,
And scho annone fell on a deidly swoun.
Seand this cais, Proserpyne maid hir boun,
Quhilk clepit is the goddes infernall,
Ontill hir court this gentill quene can call.

And quhen scho vaneist was and unwisible,
Hir madyn wepit with a wofull cheir,
Cryand with mony schowt and voce terrible,
Quhill at the last King Orpheus can heir,
And of hir cry the causs sone cowth he speir.
Scho said, "Allace, Euridicess, your quene,
Is with the phary tane befoir my ene!"

This noble king, inflammit all in yre,
And rampand as a lyoun rewanus,
With awfull luke and ene glowand as fyre,

Sperid the maner, and the maid said thuss:
"Scho strampit on a serpent venemuss
And fell on swoun - with that the quene of fary
Clawcht hir up sone and furth with hir cowth cary."

Quhen scho had said, the king sichit full soir:
His hairt neir brist for verry dule and wo,
Half out of mynd, he maid no tary moir,
Bot tuk his harp and on to wod can go
Wrinkand his handis, walkand to and fro,
Quhill he mycht stand, syne sat doun on a stone,
And till his harp thusgait he maid his mone.

"O dulfull herp with mony dully string,
Turne all thy mirth and musik in murning,
And seiss of all thy sutell songis sweit!
Now weip with me, thy lord and cairfull king,
Quhilk lossit hes in erd all his lyking,
And all thy game thow change in gole and greit!
Thy goldin pynnis with mony teiris weit,
And all my pane for till report thow preiss,
Cryand with me in every steid and streit,
`Quhair art thow gone, my luve Ewridicess?'"

Him to rejoss, yit playit he a spring,
Quhill that the fowlis of the wid can sing,

And treis dansit with thair levis grene,
Him to devod from his greit womenting;
Bot all in vane, that wailyeit him no thing,
His hairt wes so upoun his lusty quene;
The bludy teiris sprang out of his ene,
Thair wes no solace mycht his sobbing sess,
Bot cryit ay, with cairis cauld and kene,
"Quhair art thow gone, my lufe Euridicess?

"Fair weill, my place; fair weill, plesandis and play;
And wylcum, woddis wyld and wilsum way,
My wicket werd in wildirnes to ware!
My rob ryell and all my riche array
Changit sal be in rude russet and gray;
My dyademe in till a hate of hair;
My bed sal be with bever, brok, and bair,
In buskis bene, with mony busteouss bess,
Withouttin song, sayand with siching sair,
`Quhair art thow gone, my luve Euridicess?'

"I the beseik, my fair fader Phebuss,
Haif pety of thy awin sone Orpheuss;
Wait thow nocht weill I am thy sone and chyld?
Now heir my plaint, peinfull and peteuss;
Direk me fro this deid so doloruss,
Quhilk gois thus withouttin gilt begyld;

Lat nocht thy face with cluddis to be oursyld;
Len me thy lycht and lat me nocht go leiss
To find that fair in fame that was nevir fyld,
My lady quene and lufe, Euridicess!

"O Jupiter, thow god celestiall,
And grantschir to my self, on the I call
To mend my murning and my drery mone;
Thou gif me forss that I nocht fant nor fall
Till I hir fynd, forsuth seik hir I sall,
And nowthir stint nor stand for stok nor stone!
Throw thy godheid, gyde me quhair scho is gone;
Gar hir appeir, and put my hairt in pess!"
King Orpheuss thus with his harp allone
Sore wepit for his wyf Erudices.

Quhen endit wer thir songis lamentable,
He tuk his harp and on his breist can hing;
Syne passit to the hevin, as sayis the fable,
To seik his wyfe - bot that welyeid no thing.
By Wedlingis Streit he went, but tareing,
Syne come doun throw the speir of Saturne ald,
Quhilk fader is to all the stormis cald.

Quhen scho wes soucht outhrow that cauld regioun,
Till Jupiter, his grandschir, can he wend,

Quhilk rewit soir his lamentatioun,
And gart his spheir be socht fro end to end;
Scho was nocht thair; and doun he can descend
Till Mars, the god of batell and of stryfe,
And socht his spheir; yit gat he nocht his wyfe.

Than went he doun till his fadir Phebus,
God of the sone, with bemis brycht and cleir;
Bot quhen he saw his awin sone Orpheuss
In sic a plicht, that changit all his cheir.
He gart annone ga seik throw all his spheir,
Bot all in vane, his lady come nocht thair.
He tuk his leif and to Venus can fair.

Quhen he hir saw, he knelit and said thuss:
"Wait ye nocht weill I am your awin trew knycht?
In luve none leler than schir Orpheuss,
And ye of luve goddass, and most of micht,
Of my lady help me to get a sicht!"
"For suth," quod scho, "ye mone seik nedirmair."
Than fra Venus he tuk his leif but mair.

Till Mercury but tary is he gone,
Quhilk callit is the god of eloquens;
Bot of his wyf thair gat he knawlege none.
Wyth wofull hairt he passit doun frome thens;

On to the mone he maid na residens;
Thus from the hevin he went onto the erd,
Yit be the way sum melody he lerd.

In his passage amang the planeitis all,
He hard a hevinly melody and sound,
Passing all instrumentis musicall,
Causit be rollyn of the speiris round;
Quhilk armony, of all this mappamound,
Quhilk moving seiss, unyt perpetuall -
Quhilk of this warld Plato the saul can call.

Thare leirit he tonis proportionat,
As duplare, triplare, and epetritus;
Enolius, and eik the quadruplait;
Epoddeus, rycht hard and curius;
Off all thir sex, sueite and delicius,
Rycht consonant, fyfe hevinly symphonyss
Componyt ar, as clerkis can devyse.

First diatesserone, full sueit I wiss;
And dyapasone, semple and duplate;
And dyapenty, componyt with the dyss;
Thir makis fyve, of thre multiplicat.
This mirry musik and mellefluat,
Compleit and full of nummeris od and evin,

Is causit be the moving of the hevin.

Off sic musik to wryt I do bot doit,
Thairfor of this mater a stray I lay,
For in my lyfe I cowth nevir sing a noit;
Bot I will tell how Orpheus tuk the way
To seik his wyfe attour the gravis gray;
Hungry and cauld, our mony wilsum wone,
Withouttin gyd, he and his harp allone.

He passit furth the space of twenty dayis,
Fer and full fer and ferrer than I can tell,
And ay he fand streitis and reddy wayis,
Till at the last unto the get of hell
He come, and thair he fand a porter fell,
With thre heidis, was callit Serberus;
A hound of hell, a monstour mervellus.

Than Orpheus began to be agast
Quhen he beheld that ugly hellis hound;
He tuk his harp and on it playit fast,
Till at the last, throw sueitnes of the sound,
The dog slepit and fell doun on the ground,
And Orpheus attour his wame in stall,
And neddirmair he went, as ye heir sall.

Than come he till a rywir wonder depe,
Our it a brig, and on it sisteris thre,
Quhilk had the entré of the brig to keip:
Electo, Mygra, and Thesaphone,
Turnit a quheill wes ugly for to se,
And on it spred a man hecht Ixione,
Rolland about rycht windir wo begone.

Than Orpheus playd a joly spring;
The thre susteris full fast thay fell on sleip;
The ugly quheill seisit of hir quhirling;
Thus left wes none the entré for to keip.
Thane Ixion out of the quheill gan creip
And stall away; and Orpheus annone
Without stopping atour the brig is gone.

Syne come he till a wonder grisely flude,
Drubly and deip, that rythly doun can rin,
Quhair Tantelus nakit full thristy stude,
And yit the wattir yede aboif his chin;
Quhen he gaipit, thair wald no drop cum in;
Quhen he dowkit, the watter wald discend;
Thus gat he nocht his thrist to slake nor mend.

Befoir his face ane apill hang also,
Fast at his mouth, upoun a twynid threde;

Quhen he gaipit, it rollit to and fro
And fled as it refusit him to feid.
Quhen Orpheus thus saw him suffir neid,
He tuk his harp and fast on it can clink:
The wattir stud, and Tantalus gat a drink.

Syne ovr a mure with thornis thik and scherp,
Wepand allone, a wilsum way he went,
And had nocht bene throw suffrage of his harp,
With fell pikis he had bene schorne and schent;
As he blenkit besyd hym on the bent,
He saw lyand speldit a wofull wicht,
Nalit full fast, and Titius he hecht.

And on his breist thair sat a grisly grip,
Quhilk with his bill his belly throw can boir,
Both maw, myddret, hart, lever, and trip
He ruggit out; his panis was the moir.
Quhen Orpheus thus saw him this suffir soir,
He tuke his herp and maid sueit melody;
The grip is fled, and Titius left his cry.

Beyond this mure he fand a feirfull streit,
Myrk as the nycht, to pass rycht dengerus -
For sliddreness skant mycht he hald his feit -

In quhilk thair wes a stynk rycht odiuss
That gydit him to hiddouss hellis hous,
Quhair Rodomantus and Proserpina
Wer king and quene; and Orpheus in can ga.

O dully place and grundles deip dungeoun,
Furnes of fyre and stink intollerable,
Pit of dispair without remissioun;
Thy meit wennome, thy drink is pusonable,
Thy grit panis to compte unnumerable;
Quhat creature cumis to dwell in the
Is ay deand, and nevirmoir sall de.

Thair fand he mony cairfull king and quene,
With croun on heid with brass full birnand,
Quhilk in thair lyfe rycht maisterful had bene
And conquerouris of gold, richess, and land:
Hectore of Troy and Priame thair he fand,
And Alexander for his wrang conqueist,
Antiochus als for his foull incest,

And Julius Cesar for his foull crueltee,
And Herod wyth his brudiris wyfe he saw,
And Nero for his grit iniquitie,
And Pilot for his breking of the law;
Syne undir that he lukit and cowth knaw

Cresus that king, none mychtiar on mold,
For cuvatyse yet full of birnand gold.

Thair saw he Pharo, for the oppressioun
Of Godis folk, on quhilk the plaigis fell;
And Sawll for the grit abusioun
Of Justice to the folk of Israell;
Thair saw he Acob and quene Jesabell,
Quhilk silly Nabot that was a propheit trew,
For his wyne yaird withouttin mercy slew.

Thair saw he mony paip and cardynall,
In haly kirk quhilk did abusioun;
And bischopis in thair pontificall
Be symonie and wrang intrusioun;
Abbottis and all men of religioun,
For evill disponyng of thair place and rent,
In flame of fyre wer bittirly torment.

Syne neddirmair he went quhair Pluto was
And Proserpyne, and thiderward he drew,
Ay playand on his harp quhair he cowth pass,
Till at the last Erudices he knew,
Lene and deidlyk, peteouss paill of hew,
Rycht warsche and wane and walluid as the weid,
Hir lilly lyre was lyk unto the leid.

Quod he, "My lady leill and my delyt,
Full wo is me to se yow changit thus.
Quhair is your rude as ross wyth cheikis quhyte,
Your cristell ene with blenkis amorus,
Your lippis reid to kiss delicius?"
Quod scho, "As now I der nocht tell, perfay,
Bot ye sall wit the causs ane uthir day."

Quod Pluto, "Schir, thocht scho be lyk ane elf,
Scho hes no causs to plenye, and for quhy?
Scho fairis alsweill daylie as dois my self,
Or king Herod, for all his chevelry.
It is langour that putis hir in sic ply;
War scho at hame in hir cuntré of Trace,
Scho wald rewert full sone in fax and face."

Than Orpheus befoir Pluto sat doun,
And in his handis quhit his herp can ta,
And playit mony sueit proportioun,
With baiss tonys in ypodorica,
With gemilling in yporlerica;
Quhill at the last, for rewth and grit petie,
Thay weipit soir that cowth him heir or se.

Than Proserpene and Pluto bad him ass

His waresoun, and he wald haif rycht nocht,
Bot licience wyth his wyfe away to pass
To his cuntré, that he so far had socht.
Quod Proserpyne, "Sen I hir hiddir brocht,
We sall nocht pairte without conditioun."
Quod he, "Thairto I mak promissioun."

"Eruidices than be the hand thow tak,
And pass thi way, bot undirneth this pane:
Gife thow turnis, or blenkis behind thy bak,
We sall hir haif forewir till hell agane."
Thocht this was hard, yit Orpheus was fane,
And on thay went, talkand of play and sport,
Till thay almost come to the outwart port.

Thus Orpheus, with inwart lufe repleit,
So blindit was with grit effectioun,
Pensyfe apon his wyf and lady sueit.
Remembrit nocht his hard conditioun.
Quhat will ye moir? In schort conclusioun,
He blent bakwart and Pluto come annone,
And on to hell with hir agane is gone.

Allace, it was grit pety for to heir
Of Orpheus the weping and the wo,
How his lady, that he had bocht so deir,

Bot for a luk so sone wes tane him fro.

Flatlingis he fell and micht no fordir go,

And lay a quhyle in swoun and extasy;

Quhen he ourcome, this out of lufe can cry:

"Quhat art thow, luve? How sall I the defyne?

Bittir and sueit, crewall and merciable;

Plesand to sum, til uthir plent and pyne;

Till sum constant, to uthir wariable;

Hard is thy law, thy bandis unbrekable;

Quho servis the, thocht thay be newir so trew,

Perchance sum tyme thay sall haif causs to rew.

"Now find I weill this proverb trew," quod he,

"Hart on the hurd, and handis on the soir;

Quhair luve gois, on fors mone turne the e.'

I am expart, and wo is me thairfoir;

Bot for a luke my lady is forloir."

Thus chydand on with luve, our burne and bent,

A wofull wedo hamewart is he went.

Moralitas fabule sequitur

Lo, wirthy folk, Boece, that senatour,

To wryt this fenyeit fable tuk in cure,

In his gay buke of consolatioun,
For our doctrene and gud instructioun;
Quhilk in the self, suppoiss it fenyeid be,
And hid under the cloik of poetré,
Yit maister Trivat, doctour Nicholass,
Quhilk in his tyme a noble theologe wass,
Applyis it to gud moralitie,
Rycht full of fructe and seriositie.

Fair Phebus is the god of sapience;
Caliope, his wyfe, is eloquence;
Thir twa mareit gat Orpheus belyfe,
Quhilk callit is the pairte intellectyfe
Off manis saule and undirstanding, fre
And separat fra sensualitie.
Euridices is our effectioun,
Be fantesy oft movit up and doun;
Quhile to ressone it castis the delyte,
Quhile to the flesche it settis the appetyte.
Arestius, this hird that cowth persew
Euridices, is nocht bot gud vertew,
That bissy is to keip our myndis clene;
Bot quhen we fle outthrow the medow grene,
Fra vertew till this warldis vane plesans,
Myngit with cair and full of variance,
The serpentis stang: that is the deidly syn

That posownis the saule without and in;
And than is deid and eik oppressit doun
Till warldly lust and all our affectioun.
Thane perfyte wisdome weipis wondir soir,
Seand thus gait our appetyte misfair,
And passis up to the hevyn belyve,
Schawand to us the lyfe contemplatyfe,
The perfyte wit, and eik the fervent luve
We suld haif allway to the hevin abuve.
Bot seildin thair our appetyte is fundin,
It is so fast within the body bundin;
Thairfoir dounwart we cast our myndis e,
Blindit with lust, and may nocht upwartis fle.
Sould our desyre be socht up in the spheiris,
Quhen it is tedderit in thir warldly breiris,
Quhyle on the flesch, quhyle on this warldis wrak,
And to the hevin small intent we tak?

Schir Orpheus, thou seikis all in vane
Thy wyfe so he; thairfoir cum doun agane,
And pas unto the monster mervellus
With thre heidis, that we call Cerberus,
Quhilk feinyeid is to haif so mony heidis
For to betakin thre maner of deidis.
The first is in the tendir yong bernage,
The secound deid is in the middill age,

The thrid is in greit eild quhen men ar tane;
Thus Cerberus to swelly sparis nane.
Bot quhen our mynd is myngit with sapience,
And plais upoun the herp of eloquence;
That is to say, makis persuasioun
To draw our will and our affectioun,
In every eild, fra syn and fowll delyte,
This dog our sawll na power hes to byte.

The secound monstris ar the sistiris thre:
Electo, Migera, and Thesaphany
Ar nocht ellis, in bukis as we reid,
Bot wickit thocht, evill word, and thrawart deid.
Electo is the bolling of the harte,
Mygera is the wickit word outwert,
Thesaphany is operatioun,
That makis fynall executioun
Of deidly syn; and thir thre turnis ay
The ugly quheill, quhilk is nocht ellis to say
Bot warldly men sumtyme ar castin he
Upone the quheill in gret prosperitie,
And with a quhirle, onwarly, or thai wait,
Ar thrawin doun to pure and law estait.
Of Ixione, that on the quheill wes spreid,
I sall yow tell of sum pairte, as I haif red.
He was on lyfe brukle and lecherous,

And in that craft hardy and curagus,
That he wald luve in to no lawar place
Bot Juno, quene of nature and goddace.
And on a day he went up on the sky
And socht Juno, thinkand with hir to ly:
Scho saw him cum and knew his foull intent;
A rany clud doun fra the firmament
Scho gart discend, and kest betuix thame two;
And in that clud his nature yeid him fro,
Of quhilk was generat the sentowriss,
Half man, half hors, upoun a ferly wis.
Thane for the inwart craving and offens
That Juno tuke for his grit violens,
Scho send him doun unto the sistiris thre,
Upone a quheill ay turnyt for to be.
Bot quhen ressoun and perfyte sapience
Playis upone the herp of eloquens,
And persuadis our fleschly appetyte
To leif the thocht of this warldly delyte,
Than seisis of our hert the wicket will,
Fra frawart language than the tong is still,
Our synfull deidis fallis doun on sleip,
Thane Ixione out of the quheill gan creip:
That is to say, the greit solicitud,
Quhyle up, quhyle doun, to win this warldis gud,
Seissis furthwith, and our affectioun

Waxis quiet in contemplatioun.

This Tantalus, of quhome I spak of aire,
Quhill he levit he was a gay ostlaire,
And on a nycht come travilland thairby
The god of richess, and tuk harbery
With Tantalus; and he till his supper
Slew his awin sone, that was hym leif and deir,
He gart the god eit up his flesche ilk deill
In till a sew with spycis soddin weill.
For this dispyt, quhen he was deid, annone
Was dampnit in the flud of Acherone,
Till suffer hungir, thrist, nakit and cawld,
Rycht wo begone, as I befoir haif tould.
This hungry man and thirsty, Tantalus,
Betaknis men gredy and covetouss,
The god of riches that ar ay redy
For to ressaif and tak in harbery,
And till him sieth his sone in pecis small,
That is the flesch and blud, with grit travell
To full the bag, and nevir fund in thair hairt
Upoun thame self to spend, nor tak thair pairte.
Allace, in erd quhair is thair mair foly
Than for to want, and haif haboundantly -
Till haif distress on bed, on bak and burd,
And spar till othir men of gold a hurde?

And in the nycht sleip soundly thay may nocht,
To gaddir geir so gredy is thair thocht.
Bot quhen that ressoun and intelligence
Smytis upoun the herp of conscience,
Schawand to ws quhat perrell on ilk syd
That thai incur quhay will trest or confyd
Into this warldis vane prosperitie,
Quhilk hes thir sory properteis thre,
That is to say, gottin with grit labour,
Keipit with dreid, and tynt with grit dolour -
This grit avariss be grace quha undirstud,
I trow suld leif thair grit solicitude,
And ithand thouchtis, and thair besynes
To gaddir gold and syne leif in distres;
Bot he suld drink ineuch quhen ewir hym list,
Of covatyse to slaik the birnand thrist.

This Titius lay nalit on the bent,
And wyth the grip his bowellis revin and rent;
Quhill he levit sett his entencion
To find the craft of divinatioun,
And lyrit it unto the spamen all,
To tell befoir sic thingis as wald befall;
Quhat lyfe, quhat deth, quhat destany and werd,
Provydit ware unto every man on erd.
Apollo than, for this abusioun,

Quhilk is the god of divinatioun,
For he usurpit of his facultie,
Put him to hell, and thair remanis he.
Ilk man that heiris this conclusioun
Suld dreid to serss be constillatioun
Thingis to fall undir the firmament,
Till ye or na quhilk ar indefferent,
Without profixit causis and certane,
Quhilk nane in erd may knaw bot God allane.
Quhen Orpheus upoun his harp can play
That is, our undirstanding, for to say,
Cryis, "O man, recleme thi folich harte!
Will thow be God and tak on the his parte,
To tell thingis to cum that nevir wil be,
Quhilk God hes kepit in his prevetie?
Thow ma no mair offend to God of micht,
Na with thi spaying reif fra him his richt."
This perfyte wisdome with his melody
Fleyis the spreit of fenyeid profecy,
And drawis upwart our affectioun
Fra wichcraft, spaying, and sorsery,
And superstitioun of astrology -
Saif allanerly sic maner of thingis
Quhilk upoun trew and certane caussis hingis
The quhilk mone cum, to thair causis indure,
On verry forss and nocht throw avanture,

As is the clippis and the conjunctioun
Of sone and mone, be calculatioun,
The quhilk ar fundin in trew astronomy,
Be moving of the speiris in the sky.
All thir to speik it may be tollerable,
And none udir, quhilk no caussis stable.

This ugly way, this myrk and dully streit,
Is nocht ellis bot blinding of the spreit
With myrk cluddis and myst of ignorance,
Affetterrit in this warldis vane plesance
And bissines of temporalité.
To kene the self a styme it may nocht se,
For stammeris on eftir effectioun,
Fra ill to war ale thus to hell gois doun,
That is wan howp, throw lang hanting of syn,
And fowll dispair, that mony fallis in.
Than Orpheus, our ressoun, is full wo
And twichis on his harp and biddis ho
Till our desyre and fulich appetyte,
Bidis leif this warldis full delyte.
Than Pluto god, and quene of hellis fyre,
Mone grant to ressoun on forss the desyre;
Than Orpheus hes wone Euridices,
Quhen our desyre with ressoun makis pess,
And seikis up to contemplatioun,

Of syn detestand the abutioun.
Bot ilk man suld be wyse and warly se
That he bakwart cast nocht his myndis e,
Gifand consent and delectatioun
Of fleschly lust and for the affectioun;
For thane gois bakwart to the syn agane
Our appetyte, as it befoir was slane
In warldly lust and vane prosperité,
And makis ressoun wedow for to be.

Now pray we God, sen our affectioun,
Is allway promp and reddy to fall doun,
That He wald undirput His haly hand
Of mantenans, and gife us forss to stand
In perfyte luve, as He is glorius.
And thus endis the taill of Orpheus.

The Annunciation

    Forcy as deith is likand lufe,
    Throuch quhome al bittir suet is;
    No thing is hard, as writ can pruf,
    Till him in lufe that letis;
    Luf us fra barret betis.
    Quhen fra the hevinly sete abufe
    In message Gabriell couth muf,

And with myld Mary metis,
And said, "God wele the gretis;
In the He will tak rest and rufe,
But hurt of syne or yit reprufe;
In Him sett thi decret is."

This message mervale gert that myld,
And silence held but soundis,
As weill aferit a maid infild.
The angell it expoundis,
How that hir wame but woundis
Consave it suld, fra syne exild;
And quhen this carpin wes compilit,
Brichtnes fra bufe aboundis.
Thane fell that gay to groundis,
Of Goddis grace na thing begild;
Wox in hir chaumer chaist with child,
With Crist our kyng that cround is.

Thir tithingis tauld, the messinger
Till hevin agane he glidis;
That princes pure withoutyn peir
Full plesandly applid is,
And blith with barne abidis.
O worthy wirschip singuler,
To be moder and madyn meir,

As Cristin faith confidis;
That borne was of hir sidis
Our makar, Goddis sone so deir,
Quhilk erd, wattir, and hevinnis cleir
Throw grace and virtu gidis.

The miraclis ar mekle and meit
Fra luffis ryver rynnis;
The low of luf haldand the hete
Unbrynt full blithlie birnis;
Quhen Gabriell beginnis
With mouth that gudely may to grete,
The wand of Aarone, dry but wete,
To burioun nocht blynnis;
The flesch all donk within is,
Upon the erd na drop couth fleit;
Sa was that may maid moder suete
And sakeles of all synnis.

Hir mervalus haill madinhede
God in hir bosum bracis,
And Hir divinité fra dreid
Hir kepit in all casis.
The hie God of His gracis
Him self dispisit, us to speid,
And dowtit nocht to dee on deid;

He panit for our peacis,
And with His blude us bacis,
Bot quhen He ras up, as we rede,
The cherité of His Godhede
Was plane in every placis.

O lady lele and lusumest,
Thy face moist fair and schene is;
O blosum blith and bowsumest,
Fra carnale cryme that clene is;
This prayer fra my splene is,
That all my werkis wikkitest
Thow put away and mak me chaist
Fra Termigant that teyn is,
And fra his cluke that kene is,
And syne till hevin my saule thou haist,
Quhair thi makar, of michtis mast,
Is kyng, and thow thair quene is.

The Abbey Walk

Allone as I went up and doun,
In ane abbay wes fair to se,
Thinkand quhat consolatioun
Wes best in to adversitie,

On cais I kest on syd myne e
And saw this writtin upoun a wall:
"Off quhat estait, man, that thow be,
Obey and thank thi God off all.

"Thy kindome and thy grit empyre,
Thy ryeltie nor rich array,
Sall nocht indure at thi desyre,
Bot as the wind will wend away;
Thy gold and all thi gudis gay,
Quhen fortoun list, will fra the fall:
Sen thow sic sampillis seyis ilk day,
Obey and thank thi God of all.

"Job was moist riche, in writ we find,
Thobe moist full of cheretie -
Job wox peur and Thoby blynd,
Baith temptit with adversitie:
Sen blindnes wes infirmitie,
And povertie was naturall,
Thairfoir in patience baith he and he
Obeid and thankit God of all.

"Thocht thow be blind or haif ane halt,
Or in thy face deformit ill,
Sa it cum nocht throw thy defalt,

Na man sowld the repreif by skill:
Blame nocht thy lord, sa is his will,
Spur nocht thy fute aganis the wall,
Bot with meik hairt and prayar still
Obey and thank thy God of all.

"God of His justice mon correct,
And of His mercy petie haif;
He is ane juge to nane suspect,
To puneis synffull man and saif:
Thocht thow be lord attouir the laif,
And eftirwart maid bund and thrall,
Ane peure begger with skrip and staif,
Obey and thank thy God of all.

"This changeing and grit variance
Of erdly staitis up and doun
Is nocht throw casualtie and chance,
As sum men sayis, withowt ressoun,
Bot be the grit provisioun
Of God aboif that rewill the sall:
Thairfoir evir thow mak the boun
To obey and thank thy God of all.

"In welth be meik, heiche not thy self,
Be glaid in wilfull povertie;

Thy power and thy warldlie pelf
Is nocht bot verry vanitie:
Remembir him that deit on tre
For thy saik taistit bittir gall,
Quha hyis law and lawis he -
Obey and thank thy God of all."

The Bludy Serk

This hindir yeir I hard be tald
Thair was a worthy king;
Dukis, erlis, and barronis bald
He had at his bidding;
The lord was anceane and ald
And sexty yeiris cowth ring,
He had a dochter fair to fald,
A lusty lady ying.

Off all fairheid scho bur the flour,
And eik hir faderis air,
Off lusty laitis and he honour,
Meik bot and debonair;
Scho wynnit in a bigly bour,
On fold wes none so fair,
Princis luvit hir paramour

In cuntreis our-allquhair.

Thair dwelt alyt besyde the king
A fowll gyane of ane;
Stollin he hes the lady ying,
Away with hir is gane,
And kest hir in his dungering
Quhair licht scho micht se nane;
Hungir and cauld and grit thristing
Scho fand in to hir wane.

He wes the laithliest on to luk
That on the grund mycht gang,
His nailis wes lyk ane hellis cruk,
Thairwith fyve quarteris lang;
Thair wes nane that he ovrtuk,
In rycht or yit in wrang,
Bot all in schondir he thame schuke,
The gyane wes so strang.

He held the lady day and nycht
Within his deip dungeoun,
He wald nocht gif of hir a sicht
For gold nor yit ransoun,
Bot gife the king mycht get a knycht
To fecht with his persoun,

To fecht with him both day and nycht
Quhill ane wer dungin doun.

The king gart seik baith fer and neir,
Beth be se and land,
Off ony knycht gife he micht heir
Wald fecht with that gyand;
A worthy prince that had no peir
Hes tane the deid on hand,
For the luve of the lady cleir,
And held full trew cunnand.

That prince come prowdly to the toun,
Of that gyane to heir,
And fawcht with him his awin persoun
And tuke him presoneir,
And kest him in his awin dungeoun
Allane withouttin feir,
With hungir, cauld, and confusioun,
As full weill worthy weir.

Syne brak the bour, had hame the bricht
Unto hir fadir deir;
Sa evill wondit was the knycht
That he behuvit to de;
Unlusum was his likame dicht,

His sark was all bludy;
In all the warld was thair a wicht
So peteous for to sy?

The lady murnyt and maid grit mone
With all hir mekle micht,
"I luvit nevir lufe bot one
That dulfully now is dicht.
God sen my lyfe wer fra me tone
Or I had sene yone sicht,
Or ellis in begging evir to gone
Furth with yone curtas knycht!"

He said, "Fair lady, now mone I de,
Trestly ye me trow;
Tak ye my sark that is bludy,
And hing it forrow yow;
First think on it and syne on me
Quhen men cumis yow to wow."
The lady said, "Be Mary fre,
Thairto I mak a wow!"

Quhen that scho lukit to the serk
Scho thocht on the persoun,
And prayit for him with all hir harte
That lowsd hir of bandoun,

Quhair scho was wont to sit full merk
In that deip dungeoun;
And evir quhill scho wes in quert
That was hir a lessoun.

Sa weill the lady luvit the knycht
That no man wald scho tak;
Sa suld we do our God of micht
That did all for us mak,
Quhilk fullely to deid wes dicht
For sinfull manis saik;
Sa suld we do both day and nycht,
With prayaris to him mak.

Moralitas

This king is lyk the Trinitie,
Baith in hevin and heir,
The manis saule to the lady,
The gyane to Lucefeir,
The knycht to Chryst that deit on tre
And coft our synnis deir,
The pit to hell with panis fell,
The syn to the woweir.

The lady was wowd, bot scho said nay

With men that wald hir wed;
Sa suld we wryth all syn away,
That in our breist is bred.
I pray to Jesu Chryst verrey,
For us His blud that bled,
To be our help on domysday
Quhair lawis ar straitly led.

The saule is Godis dochtir deir,
And eik his handewerk,
That was betrasit with Lucifeir
Quha sittis in hell full merk,
Borrowit with Chrystis angell cleir;
Hend men, will ye nocht herk?
For His lufe that bocht us deir,
Think on the bludy serk.

The Garmont of Gud Ladeis

Wald my gud lady lufe me best
And wirk eftir my will,
I suld ane garmond gudliest
Gar mak hir body til.

Off he honour suld be hir hud,

Upoun hir heid to weir,
Garneist with govirnance so gud,
Na demyng suld hir deir.

Hir sark suld be hir body nixt
Of chestetie so quhyt,
With schame and dreid togidder mixt
The same suld be perfyt.

Hir kirtill suld be of clene constance,
Lasit with lesum lufe,
The mailyeis of continwance,
For nevir to remufe.

Hir gown suld be of gudlines,
Weill ribband with renowne,
Purfillit with plesour in ilk place,
Furrit with fyne fassoun.

Hir belt suld be of benignitie
Abowt hir middill meit,
Hir mantill of humilitie
To tholl bayth wind and weit.

Hir hat suld be of fair having,
And hir tepat of trewth,

Hir patelet of gud pansing
Hir hals ribbane of rewth.

Hir slevis suld be of esperance
To keip hir fra dispair,
Hir gluvis of gud govirnance
To hyd hir fynyearis fair.

Hir schone suld be of sickernes
In syne that scho nocht slyd,
Hir hois of honestie, I ges,
I suld for hir provyd.

Wald scho put on this garmond gay,
I durst sweir by my seill
That scho woir nevir grene nor gray
That set hir half so weill.

Against Hasty Credence

Fals titlaris now growis up full rank,
Nocht ympit in the stok of cheretie,
Howping at thair lord to gett grit thank
Thay haif no dreid on thair nybouris to lie;
Than sowld ane lord awyse him weill I se

Quhen ony taill is brocht to his presence
Gif it be groundit in to veretie,
Or he thairto gif haistely creddence.

Ane worthy lord sowld wey ane taill wyslie,
The tailltellar, and quhome of it is tald,
Gif it be said for luve or for invy,
And gif the tailisman weill avow it wald;
Than eftirwart the pairteis sowld be cald
For thair excuse, to mak lawfull defence:
Than sowld ane lord the ballance evinly hald
And gif not at the first haistie creddence.

It is no wirschep for ane nobill lord
For fals tailis to put ane trew man doun,
And gevand creddence to the first recoird,
He will not heir his excusatioun;
The tittillaris so in his heir can roun
The innocent may get no awdience:
Ryme as it may, thair is na ressoun,
To gif till taillis hestely creddence.

Thir teltellaris oft tymes dois grit skaith,
And raissis mortall feid and discrepance,
And makis lordis with thair serwandis wreith,
And baneist be withowtin cryme perchance.

It is the grund of stryfe and all distance,

Moir perrellus than ony pestillence,

Ane lord in flatterreris to haif plesance,

Or to gif lyaris hestely creddence.

O thow wyse lord, quhen cumis a flatterrer,

The for to pleis and hurt the innocent,

Will tell ane taill of thy familiar,

Thow sowld the pairteis call incontinent,

And sitt doun sadly in to jugement,

And serche the caus weill, or thow gif sentence,

Or ellis heireftir in cais thow may repent

That thow to tailis gaif so grit creddence.

O wicket tung, sawand dissentioun,

Of fals taillis to tell that will not tyre,

Moir perrellus than ony fell pusoun,

The pane of hell thow sall haif to thi hyre;

Richt swa sall thay that hes joy or desyre

To gife thair eirris to heird with patience,

For of discord it kendillis mony fyre,

Throwch geving talis hestely creddence.

Bakbyttaris to heir it is no bowrd,

For thay ar excommunicat in everie place;

Thre personis severall he slayis with ane wowrd -

Him self, the heirar, and the man saiklace;
Within ane hude he hes ane dowbill face,
Ane bludy tung undir a fair pretence.
I say no moir, bot God grant lordis grace
To gife to taillis nocht hestely creddence.

The Praise of Age

Wythin a garth, under a rede rosere,
Ane ald man and decrepit herd I syng;
Gay was the note, suete was the voce and clere;
It was grete joy to here of sik a thing.
"And to my dome," he said in his dytyng,
"For to be yong I wald not, for my wis,
Off all this warld to mak me lord and king:
The more of age, the nerar hevynnis blis.

"False is this warld and full of variance,
Besoucht with syn and othir sytis mo;
Treuth is all tynt, gyle has the gouvernance,
Wrechitnes has wroht all welthis wele to wo,
Fredome is tynt and flemyt the lordis fro,
And covatise is all the cause of this;
I am content that youthede is ago:
The more of age, the nerar hevynnis blisse.

"The state of youth I repute for na gude,
For in that state sik perilis now I see
Bot full smal grace; the regeing of his blude
Can none gaynstand quhill that he agit be;
Syne of the thing that tofore joyit he
Nothing remaynis for to be callit his,
For quhy it were bot veray vanitee:
The more of age, the nerar hevynnis blisse.

"Suld no man traist this wrechit warld, for quhy
Of erdly joy ay sorow is the end,
The state of it can noman certify;
This day a king, to morne na gude to spend.
Quhat have we here bot grace us to defend?
The quhilk God grant us, for to mend oure mys,
That to His glore He may oure saulis send:
The more of age, the nerar hevynnis blisse."

Ane Prayer for the Pest

O eterne God of power infinyt,
To Quhois hie knawledge na think is obscure-
That is, or wes, or sal be, is perfyt
Into Thi sicht, quhill that this warld indure-

Haif mercy of us, indigent and peure;
Thow dois no wrang to punis our offens:
O lord, That is to mankynd haill succure,
Preserve us fra this perrelus pestilens!

We The beseik, O lord of lordis all,
Thy eiris inclyne and heir our grit regrait:
We ask remeid of The in generall,
That is of help and confort dissolait:
Bot Thow with rewth our hairtis recreate,
We ar bot deid, but only Thy clemens:
We The exhort on kneis law prostrait,
Preserve us from this perrellus pestilens!

We ar rycht glaid Thow punis our trespas
Be ony kynd of udir tribulatioun:
Wer it Thy will, O lord of hevin, allais,
That we suld thus be haistely put doun
And de as beistis without confessioun,
That nane dar mak with udir residens?
O blissit Jesu, that wore the thorny croun,
Preserve us frome this perrelus pestilens!

Use derth, O lord, or seiknes and hungir soir,
And slak Thy plaig that is so penetryfe:
Thy pepill ar preist - quha may remeid thairfoir,

Bot Thow, O lord, that for thame lost Thy lyfe?
Suppois our syne be to The pungetyfe,
Our deid ma na thing our synnis recompens;
Haif mercy, Lord, we may nocht with The stryfe;
Preserve us fra this perrelus pestilens!

Haif mercy, Lord; haif mercy, Hevyns King;
Haif mercy of Thy pepill penitent;
Haif mercy of our petous punissing;
Retreit the sentence and Thy just jugement
Aganis us synnaris that servis to be schent;
Without mercy we may mak no defens;
Thow that but rewth upoun the Rud wes rent,
Preserve us frome this perrellus pestilens!

Remembir, Lord, how deir Thow hes us bocht,
That for us synnaris sched Thy pretius blude;
Now to redeme that Thow hes maid of nocht,
That is of virtew barrane and denude,
Haif rewth, Lord, of Thyne awin similitude,
Punis with pety and nocht with violens;
We knaw it is for our ingratitude
That we ar puneist with this pestillens.

Thow grant us grace for till amend our mis
And till evaid this crewall suddane deid;

We knaw our sin is all the caus of this;
For opin sin thair is set no remeid;
The justice of God mon punis than be deid,
For by the law he will with nane dispens;
Quhair justice laikis thair is eternall feid
Of God, that suld preserf fra pestilens.

Bot wald the heidismen, that suld keip the law,
Punis the peple for thair transgressioun,
Thair wald na deid the peple than ourthraw;
Bot thay ar gevin sa plenly to oppressioun
That God will nocht heir thair intecessioun,
Bot all ar punist for thair inobediens
Be swerd or deid, withouttin remissioun,
And hes just caus to send us pestilens.

Superne Lucerne, guberne this pestilens,
Preserve and serve that we nocht sterf thairin,
Declyne that pyne be Thy devyne prudens,
For trewth, haif rewth, lat nocht our slewth us twyn;
Our syte, full tyte, wer we contryt, wald blin;
Dissivir did nevir, quha evir The besocht.
Send grace, with space, for to arrace fra sin;
Lat nocht be tint that Thow sa deir hes bocht!

O Prince preclair, this cair quotidiane,

We The exort, distort it in exyle;
Bot Thow remeid, this deid is bot ane trane
For to dissaif the laif and thame begyle.
Bot Thow, sa wyse, devyse to mend this byle,
Of this mischeif quha may releif us ocht
For wrangus win, bot Thow our sin oursyle?
Lat nocht be tint that Thow sa deir hes bocht!

Sen for our vice, that justice mon correct,
O king most hie, now pacifé thy feid;
Our sin is huge, refuge we nocht suspect;
As Thow art juge, dislug us of this dreid,
In tyme assent, or we be schent with deid,
For we repent all tyme mispent forthocht;
Thairfoir, evirmor, be gloir to Thy Godheid;
Lat nocht be tint that Thow sa deir hes bocht!

The Ressoning betuix Aige and Yowth

Yowth

Quhen fair Flora, the godes of the flouris,
Baith firth and feildis freschly had ourfrete,
And perly droppis of the balmy schouris
Thir widdis grene had with thair watter wete,

Movand allone in mornyng myld I mete
A mirry man, that all of mirth cowth mene,
Singand the sang that sueitly wes sete:
"O yowth, be glaid in to thi flouris grene!"

Aige

I lukit furth a litill me before:
I saw a cative on a club cumand,
With cheikis lene and lyart lokis hore;
His ene wes how, his voce wes hes hostand,
Wallowit and wan and waik as ony wand;
Ane bill he beure upoun his breist abone,
In letteres leill but les, with this legend:
"O yowth, thi flouris fedis fellone sone!"

Yowth

This yungman lap upoun the land full lycht,
And mervellit mekle of his misdum maid;
"Waddin I am," quod he, "and wonder wicht,
With bran as bair, and breist burly and braid.
Na growme on grund my gardoun may degraid,
Nor of my pith may pair half wirth a prene;
My face is fair, my figour will nocht faid:
O yowth, be glaid in to thi flouris grene!"

Aige

This senyeour sang, bot with a sobir stevin;
Schakand his berd, he said, "My bairne, lat be.
I wes within thir sexty yeiris and sevin
Ane freik on fold bayth frak, forsy, and fre;
Als glad, als gay, als yung, als yaip as ye.
Bot now that day is ordrawyne and done;
Luk thow my laythly lykyne gif I le:
O yowth, thy flouris fadis fellone sone!"

Yowth

Ane uthir vers this yungman yit cowth sing:
"At luvis law a quhyle I think to leite,
In court to cramp clenely in my clething
And luke amangis thir lusty ladeis sueit;
Of marriege to mell with mowis meit,
In secreitnes quhair we may nocht be sene,
And so with birdis blythlie my baillis beit:
O yowth, be glaid in to thi flowris grene!"

Aige

This austryne man gaif ansuer angirly:

"For thi crampyn thow sall bayth cruk and cowr,
And thy fleschely lust thow sall defy,
And pane the sall put fra parramour -
Than will no bird be blyth of the in bour,
Quhen thi manheid sall move as the mone;
Thow sall assay gif that my sang be sour:
O yowth, thy flouris fadis fellone sone!"

Yowth

This myrry man of mirth yit movit moir:
"My cors is clene without corruptioun,
My self is sound, but seiknes or but soir,
My wittis fyve in dew proportioun,
My curage is of clene complexioun,
My hairt is haill, my lever, and my splene;
Thairfoir to reid this rowll I haif ressoun:
O yowth, be glaid in to thy flouris grene!"

Aige

This bevir hair said to this berly berne:
"This breif thow sall obey, sone, be thow bald;
Thy stait, thi strenth thocht it be stark and sterne,
The feviris fell and eild sall gar the fald;
Thy corpis sall clyng, thi curagis sall wax cald,

The heill sall hynk and tak a hurt bot hone;
Thy wittis fyve sall wane, thocht thow not wald;
O yowth, thi flouris fadis fellone sone!"

Yowth

This galyart grutchit and began to greif,
And on his wayis wrechitly he went but wene;
This lene man luche na thing bot tuk his leif,
And I abaid ondir the levis grene.
Off the cedullis the suth quhen I had sene,
On trewth, me thocht thai trevist in thair tone:
"O yowth, be glaid in to thi flouris grene!"
"O yowth, thi flouris fedis fellone sone!"

The Ressoning betuix Deth and Man

Deth

"O mortall man, behold, tak tent to me,
Quhilk sowld thi mirrour be baith day and nycht.
All erdly thing that evir tuik lyfe mon die:
Paip, empriour, king, barroun, and knycht,
Thocht thay be in thair roall stait and hicht,
May nocht ganestand quhen I pleiss schute this derte;

Waltownis, castellis, and towiris nevir so wicht

May nocht risist quhill it be at his herte."

Man

"Now quhat art thow that biddis me thus tak tent

And mak ane mirrour day and nycht of the,

Or with thy dert I sowld richt soir repent?

I trest trewly off that thow sall sone lie.

Quhat freik on fold sa bald dar maniss me,

Or with me fecht, owthir on fute or horss?

Is non so wicht or stark in this cuntré,

Bot I sall gar him bow to me on fors."

Deth

"My name, at me forswth sen that thou speiris,

Tha call me Deid, suthly I the declair,

Calland all man and woman to thair beiris

Quhen evir I pleiss, quhat tyme, quhat plais, or quhair.

Is nane sa stowt, sa fresche, nor yit sa fair,

Sa yung, so ald, so riche, nor yit sa peur;

Quhair evir I pass, owthir lait or air,

Mon put thame haill on forss undir my cure."

Man

"Sen it is so that nature can so wirk

That yung and awld, with riche and peure, mon die,

In my yowtheid, allace, I wes full irk,

Cowld not tak tent to gyd and governe me

Ay gude to do, fra evill deidis to fle,

Trestand ay yowtheid wold with me ay abyde,

Fulfilland evir my sensualitie

In deidly syn and specialy in pryd."

Deth

"Thairfoir repent and remord thi conscience,

Think on thir wirdis I now upoun the cry:

O wrechit man, O full of ignorance,

All thi plesance thow sall deir aby;

Dispone thy self and cum with me in hy,

Edderis, askis, and wormis meit for to be;

Cum quhen I call; thow may, me nocht denny,

Thocht thow wer paip, empriour, and king al thre."

Man

"Sen it is sua fra the I may not chaip,

This wrechit warld for me heir I defy,

And to the, Deid, to luke undir thi caip,

I offer me with hairt, richt hummilly,
Beseikand God, the Divill, my ennemy,
No power haif my sawill till assay.
Jesus, on the with peteous voce I cry,
Mercy on me to haif on Domisday."

Robene and Makyne

Robene sat on gud grene hill
Kepand a flok of fe;
Mirry Makyne said him till,
"Robene, thow rew on me!
I haif the lovit lowd and still
Thir yeiris two or thre;
My dule in dern bot gif thow dill,
Dowtles but dreid I de."

Robene anserit, "Be the Rude,
Na thing of lufe I knaw,
Bot keipis my scheip undir yone wid;
Lo quhair thay raik on raw.
Quhat hes marrit the in thy mude,
Makyne, to me thow schaw,
Or quhat is lufe, or to be lude?
Fane wald I leir that law."

"At luvis lair gife thow will leir,
Tak thair ane A B C:
Be heynd, courtas, and fair of feir,
Wyse, hardy, and fre,
So that no denger do the deir,
Quhat dule in dern thow dre;
Preis the with pane at all poweir,
Be patient and previe."

Robene anserit hir agane,
"I wait nocht quhat is luve,
Bot I haif mervell in certane
Quhat makis the this wanrufe.
The weddir is fair and I am fane,
My scheip gois haill aboif;
And we wald play, us in this plane,
Thay wald us bayth reproif."

"Robene, tak tent unto my taill
And wirk all as I reid,
And thow sall haif my hairt all haill,
Eik and my madinheid.
Sen God sendis bute for baill,
And for murning remeid,
I dern with the bot gif I daill,
Dowtles I am bot deid."

"Makyne, to morne this ilk a tyde,
And ye will meit me heir,
Peraventure my scheip ma gang besyd
Quhill we haif liggit full neir.
Bot mawgré haif I and I byd,
Fra thay begin to steir;
Quhat lyis on hairt I will nocht hyd,
Makyn, than mak gud cheir."

"Robene, thow reivis me roif and rest;
I luve bot the allone."
"Makyne, adew, the sone gois west,
The day is neir hand gone."
"Robene, in dule I am so drest
That lufe wilbe my bone."
"Ga lufe, Makyne, quhair evir thow list,
For lemman I bid none."

"Robene, I stand in sic a styll;
I sicht, and that full sair.
`Makyne, I haif bene heir this quhyle;
At hame God gif I wair."
"My huny Robene, talk ane quhyll,
Gif thow will do na mair."
"Makyne, sum uthir man begyle,

For hamewart I will fair."

Robene on his wayis went,
Als licht as leif of tre;
Mawkin murnit in hir intent,
And trowd him nevir to se.
Robene brayd attour the bent;
Than Mawkyne cryit on hie,
"Now ma thow sing, for I am schent;
Quhat alis lufe at me?"

Mawkyne went hame withowttin faill,
Full wery eftir cowth weip.
Than Robene in a ful fair daill
Assemblit all his scheip;
Be that, sum pairte of Mawkynis aill
Outthrow his hairt cowd creip.
He fallowit hir fast thair till assaill,
And till hir tuke gude keip:

"Abyd, abyd, thow fair Makyne
A word for ony thing!
For all my luve it salbe thyne,
Withowttin depairting:
All haill thy harte for till haif myne
Is all my cuvating;

My scheip to morne quhill houris nyne
Will neid of no keping."

"Robene, thow hes hard soung and say
In gestis and storeis auld,
'The man that will nocht quhen he may
Sall haif nocht quhen he wald.'
I pray to Jesu every day,
Mot eik thair cairis cauld
That first preisis with the to play,
Be firth, forrest, or fawld."

"Makyne, the nicht is soft and dry,
The wedder is warme and fair,
And the grene woid rycht neir us by
To walk attour all quhair;
Thair ma na janglour us espy,
That is to lufe contrair:
Thairin, Makyne, bath ye and I,
Unsene we ma repair."

"Robene, that warld is all away
And quyt brocht till ane end,
And nevir agane thairto perfay
Sall it be as thow wend,
For of my pane thow maid it play,

And all in vane I spend;
As thow hes done, sa sall I say,
`Murne on, I think to mend.'"

"Mawkyne, the howp of all my heill,
My hairt on the is sett,
And evirmair to the be leill
Quhill I may leif but lett;
Nevir to faill as uthiris feill,
Quhat grace that evir I gett."
"Robene, with the I will nocht deill;
Adew, for thus we mett."

Malkyne went hame blyth annewche,
Attour the holttis hair;
Robene murnit and Malkyne lewche;
Scho sang, he sichit sair;
And so left him bayth wo and wewche,
In dolour and in cair,
Kepand his hird under a huche,
Amangis the holtis hair.

Sum Practysis of Medecyne

Guk guk, gud day, ser! Gaip quhill ye get it.

Sic greting may gane weill; gud laik in your hude.
Ye wald deir me I trow, becaus I am dottit,
To ruffill me with a ryme - na, ser, be the rude.
Your saying I haif sene and on syd set it,
As geir of all gaddering, glaikit nocht gude;
Als your medicyne by mesour I haif meit met it,
The quhilk I stand ford ye nocht understude,
Bot wrett on as ye culd to gar folk wene
For feir my longis wes flaft,
Or I wes dottit or daft:
Gife I can ocht of the craft,
Heir be it sene.

Becaus I ken your cunnyng in to cure
Is clowtit and clampit and nocht weill cleird,
My prettik in pottingary ye trow be als pure
And lyk to your lawitnes - I schrew thame that leid.
Is nowdir fevir nor fell that ovr the feild fure,
Seiknes nor sairnes, in tyme gif I seid,
Bot I can lib thanne and leiche thame fra lame and lesure,
With salvis thame sound mak: on your saule beid,
That ye be sicker of this sedull I send yow,
With the suthfast seggis
That glean all egeis
With dia and dreggis
Of malis to mend yow.

Dia culcakit

Cape cuk maid, and crop the colleraige,
Ane medecyne for the maw and ye cowth mak it
With sueit satlingis and sowrokis, the sop of the sege,
The crud of my culome, with your teith crakit,
Lawrean and linget seid and the luffage,
The hair of the hurcheoun nocht half deill hakkit,
With the snowt of ane selch, ane swelling to swage:
This cure is callit in our craft dia culcakkit.
Put all thir in ane pan with pepper and pik.
Syne sett in to this
The count of ane cow kis;
Is nocht bettir I wis,
For the collik.

Dia longum

Recipe thre ruggis of the reid ruke,
The gant of ane gray meir, the claik of ane gus,
The dram of ane drekters, the douk of ane duke,
The gaw of ane grene dow, the leg of ane lows,
Fyve unce of ane fle wing, the fyn of ane fluke,
With ane sleiffull of slak that growis in the slus;
Myng all thir in ane mas with the mone cruke.

This untment is rycht ganand for your awin us,

With reid nettill seid in strang wesche to steip,

For to bath your ba cod,

Quhen ye wald nop and nod;

Is nocht bettir be God,

To latt yow to sleip.

Dia glaconicon

This dia is rycht deir and denteit in daill,

Caus it is trest and trew: thairfoir that ye tak

Sevin sobbis of ane selche, the quhidder of ane quhaill,

The lug of ane lempet is nocht to forsaik,

The harnis of ane haddok, hakkit or haill,

With ane bustfull of blude of the scho bak,

With ane brewing caldrun full of hait caill,

For it wilbe the softar and sweittar of the smak:

Thair is nocht sic ane lechecraft fra Lawdian to Lundin

It is clippit in our cannon

Dia glecolicon,

For till fle awaye fon

Quhair fulis ar fundin.

Dia custrum

The ferd feisik is fyne and of ane felloun pryce,

Gud for haising and hosting or heit at the hairt.

Recipe thre sponfull of the blak spyce,

With ane grit gowpene of the gowk fart,

The lug of ane lyoun, the gufe of ane gryce,

Ane unce of ane oster poik at the nethir parte,

Annoyntit with nurice doung for it is rycht nyce,

Myngit with mysdirt and with mustart.

Ye may clamp to this cure, and ye will mak cost,

Bayth the bellox of ane brok,

With thre crawis of the cok,

The schadow of ane yule stok,

Is gud for the host.

Gud nycht, guk guk, for sa I began;

I haif no come at this tyme langer to tary,

Bot luk on this lettir and leird gif ye can,

The prectik and poyntis of this pottingary:

Ser, minister this medecyne at evin to sum man

And or pryme be past, my powder I pary,

Thay sall blis yow or ellis bittirly yow ban,

For it sall fle thame in faith out of the fary.

Bot luk quhen ye gadder thir gressis and gers,

Outhir sawrand or sour,

That it be in ane gude oure:

It is ane mirk mirrour,

Ane uthir manis ers.

The Three Deid Pollis

O sinfull man, in to this mortall se,
Quhilk is the vaill of murnyng and of cair,
With gaistly sicht behold oure heidis thre,
Oure holkit ene, oure peilit pollis bair.
As ye ar now, in to this warld we wair,
Als fresche, als fair, als lusty to behald:
Quhan thow lukis on this suth examplair
Off thy self, man, thow may be richt unbald.

For suth it is that every man mortall
Mon suffer deid and de, that lyfe hes tane;
Na erdly stait aganis deid ma prevaill;
The hour of deth and place is uncertane,
Quhilk is referrit to the hie God allane.
Heirfoir haif mynd of deth, that thow mon dy:
This sair exampill to se quotidiane
Sowld caus all men fra wicket vycis fle.

O wantone yowth, als fresche as lusty May,
Farest of flowris, renewit quhyt and reid,
Behald our heidis, O lusty gallandis gay;
Full laithly thus sall ly thy lusty heid,
Holkit and how, and wallowit as the weid;
Thy crampand hair and eik thy cristall ene

Full cairfully conclud sall dulefull deid;
Thy example heir be us it may be sene.

O ladeis quhyt, in claithis corruscant,
Poleist with perle and mony pretius stane,
With palpis quhyt and hals so elegant
Sirculit with gold and sapheris mony ane;
Your finyearis small, quhyt as quhailis bane,
Arrayit with ringis and mony rubeis reid:
As we ly thus, so sall ye ly ilk ane,
With peilit pollis, and holkit thus your heid.

O wofull pryd, the rute of all distres,
With humill hairt upoun our pollis pens;
Man, for thy mis, ask mercy with meiknes;
Aganis deid na man may mak defens:
The empriour, for all his excellens,
King and quene, and eik all erdly stait,
Peure and riche, salbe but differens
Turnit in as and thus in erd translait.

This questioun, quha can obsolve, lat see,
Quhat phisnamour or perfyt palmester -
Quha was farest or fowlest of us thre,
Or quhilk of us of kin was gentillar,
Or maist expert in science or in lare,

In art, musik, or in astronomye?
Heir sowld be your study and repair,
And think as thus all your heidis mon be.

O febill aige, drawand neir the dait
Of dully deid, and hes thy dayis compleit,
Behald our heidis with murning and regrait,
Fall on thy kneis, ask grace at God, and greit,
With orisionis and haly salmes sweit
Beseikand him on the to haif mercy,
Now of our sawlis, bydand the decreit
Of His Godheid, to rew and glorifé.

Als we exhort that every man mortall,
For His saik that maid of nocht all thing,
For mercy cry and pray in generall
To Jesus Chryst, of hevin and erd the king,
Throwch your prayar that we and ye may ring
With the hie Fader be eternitie,
The Sone alswa, the Haly Gaist conding,
Thre knit in ane be perfyt unitie.

The Want of Wyse Men

Me mervellis of this grete confusion;
I wald sum clerk of connyng walde declerde,

Quhat gerris this warld be turnyt upsyd doun.
Thare is na faithfull fastnes founde in erd;
Now are noucht thre may traistly trow the ferde;
Welth is away, and wit is worthin wrynkis;
Now sele is sorow this is a wofull werde,
Sen want of wyse men makis fulis to sit on binkis.

That tyme quhen levit the king Saturnus,
For gudely gouvernance this warld was goldin cald;
For untreuth we wate noucht quhare to it turnis;
The tyme that Octaviane, the monarch, coud hald,
Our all was pes, wele set as hertis wald:
Than regnyt reule, and resone held his rynkis;
Now lakkis prudence, nobilitee is thralde,
Sen want of wyse men makis fulis to sitt on bynkis.

Arestotill for his moralitee,
Austyn, or Ambrose, for dyvine scripture,
Quha can placebo, and noucht half dirige,
That practik for to pike and pill the pure,
He sall cum in, and thay stand at the dure;
For warldly wyn sik walkis, quhen wysar wynkis;
Wit takis na worschip, sik is the aventure,
Sen want of wysemen makis fulis to sitt on binkis.

Now, but defense, rycht lyis all desolate,

Rycht, na resone under na rufe has rest;
Youth his but raddour, and age is obystynate,
Mycht but mercy, the pore ar all opprest.
Lerit folk suld tech the peple of the best,
Thouch lare be lytil, fer lesse in tham sinkis:
It may noucht be this warld ay thus suld lest,
That want of wyse men makis fulis sitt on binkis.

For now is exilde all ald noble corage,
Lautee, lufe, and liberalitee;
Now is stabilitee fundyn in na stage,
Nor degest connsele wyth sad maturitee;
Peas is away, all in perplexitee;
Prudence and policy ar banyst our al brinkis:
This warld is uer, sa may it callit be,
That want of wisemen makis fulis sitt on bynkis.

Quhare is the balance of just and equitee?
Nouthir meryt is preisit, na punyst is trespas;
All ledis lyvis lawles at libertee,
Noucht reulit be reson, mare than ox or asse;
Gude faith is flemyt, worthin fraellar than glas;
Trew lufe is loren, and lautee haldis no lynkis;
Sik gouvernance I call noucht worth a fasse,
Sen want of wise men makis fulis sitt on binkis.
Now wrang hes warrane, and law is bot wilfulness;

Quha hes the war is worthin on him all the wyte,

For trewth is tressoun, and faith is fals fekilness;

Gylle is now gyd, and vane lust is also delyte;

Kirk is contempnit, thay compt nocht cursing a myte;

Grit God is grevit, that me rycht soir forthinkis:

The caus of this ony man may sone wit,

That want of wysemen garis fulis sit on binkis.

Lue hes tane leif, and wirschip hes no udir wane;

With passing poverty pryd is importable;

Vyce is bot vertew, wit is with will soir ourgane;

As lairdis so laddis, daly chengeable;

But ryme or ressone all is bot heble hable;

Sic sturtfull stering in to Godis neiss it stinkis;

Bot he haif rew, all is unremedable,

For want of wise men makis fulis sit on binkis.

O lord of lordis, God and gouvernour,

Makar and movar, bath of mare and lesse,

Quhais power, wisedome, and honoure,

Is infynite, sal be, and ewir wes,

As in the principall mencioun of the messe,

All thir sayd thingis reforme as thou best thinkis;

Quhilk ar degradit, for pure pitee redresse,

Sen want of wise men makis fulis sit in binkis.

Printed in Great Britain
by Amazon